"Woodland Angels"

Where magic, mystery, and life take flight

An inspiring life guide for children and adults

By: Jennifer Bryant
Kid Tested and Approved * by Aaliyah

Acknowledgments

Dedication

I dedicate this book to my entire family, and all the children mentioned who have entrusted me with their most challenging moments.
I am so grateful for the magical presence that each one of you share in the circle of life.

I extend a spiritual acknowledgment to Cindy Westmoreland, who provided the sentimental Angel images and shared her light with everyone she met. At 92 years old, she shines more of her child's heart than anyone I know. Thank you for helping so many people shine both here and beyond - especially me.

Blessings to all who help restore the hearts of children.

Use

The most effective way to read "Woodland Angels" is one chapter at a time. This process opens the reader to an expanded understanding of the life messages within the book. Reading at a slow pace also allows the reader to connect, absorb, and process the information on a personal level.

The content speaks to all ages. It is a wonderful tool for familial communications and deepening relationships overall.

Children and adults often experience fear, family upsets, identity confusion, bullying, peer pressure, death, and other upsetting things. "Woodland Angels" subtly address these situations in a light-hearted, deeply supportive manner by re-enforcing the positive mind and faith in Spirit.

"Woodland Angels" brings forth a positive focus and self-empowerment relating to challenging life experiences and promotes honoring the self with genuineness, love, kindness, and joy.

As one's very own book of life, "Woodland Angels" continues to help guide readers as they grow and mature.

Copyright© - June 2021. Jennifer A. Bryant
All rights reserved.

Isbn: 978-1-7372790-0-6
Breath of Spirit Publishing

Contents

<u>Page</u>   <u>Content</u>

11   Rocks and Tree Tops

15   Just Wondering about Life

22   Into the Wise Woods
      The Ryan Earthworms

29   The Shadow Dancers

35   Forest Lights
      The Makaiya Ladybugs

41   The Woods Come Alive
      The Jessica Fairies
      The Brooklyn Bunnies
      The Payton Flowers
      The Jacob Glow-worms

50   Wishes and Mysteries
        The Rylee Doves
        The Jonah Honey Bees

56   A Forest Monster? Ha!

63   The Magical Women of the Forest
        The Allison Raccoon's
        The Emily Foxes

72   A New World
        The Aaliyah Butterflies
        The Miranda Ruby Phoenix

81   A Basket Full of Mysteries
        The Todderic Turkeys
        The Adamcarl Owl

88   Just Knowing Things
        The Sophia Deer
        Lauralisa Mother Universe

96   A Universe of Memory Dust
        The Shawnshawn Squirrels
        The Angel Doodlekobi

107   The Keepers of the Spirit
        The Earth Spirit Geri
        The Air Spirit Jennifer
        The Water Spirit Boni
        The Fire Spirit Faith

115   The Mighty Wizard, Mitch

124   The Super Angels
        The Archangel Raphael
        The Archangel Gabriel
        The Archangel Uriel
        The Archangel Michael

137   We Bid the Farewell

147   Drawing and Coloring Forest Friends

Introduction

For children, adults, and even animals, too - the world can sometimes feel like being lost in the woods of a forest.
There are so many mysterious things you meet and see - And so many people who are different from you.

Some people may be kind and happy - And others may be Icky and blue.
And some people can even be a little dark and scary - with the things they say and do!

But, Have No Fear
Angels are always near!

As two friends journey through the woods - they meet many new woodland friends and some pretty cool Angels, too - who share their wisdom about life, being a good person, and how to not feel icky and blue.

These magical friends want you to stay just the way you were born... happy, loving, and true. After all, if everyone in the world stayed that way - No one would ever feel yucky, alone, or afraid!

Being icky and blue is quite silly, you see - because we really only feel that way when we are believing it's true!
But, we don't ever have to feel yucky and down, if we just remember -
There are Angels all around!

In this story, you will hear many wise things about yourself, life, and people.

You will meet The Magical Woman of the Forest with her fairy dust flying all around -And the cuuuutest, little forest friends, gather from afar - to show you just how wonderful and smart you really are!

Oh, yes, of course! There is a Magical Wizard too - who puts on quite a show helping you know the magic you have inside.
Oh yes, yes - there is magic in these woods! - And amazing Angels too!
Oh, Won't you come into the forest?

Let's journey through the woods together and see - just what the Woodland Angels have to say to you and me!

This Magical Story is about Two Beautiful Children

An amazing little girl named

Whitney ~

And an awesome little boy named

Grayson!

Rocks and Treetops

Whitney and Grayson were very best friends.
And I mean the best-est, best-est friends ever!
They were always so happy, kind, and loving with each other.

They were not ever mean - And they didn't get mad at each other.
They just looooved being together.

They especially loved playing outside - exploring the earth and nature.
So, every day after school - they would walk down to the river.
They would just go walking around searching for cool things -
like rocks - and trees - and cool looking bugs, and stuff like that.

Whitney loved looking for rocks. Especially the ones that had lots of lines, colors, and different shapes.
She loved how the rocks felt in her hand - And how they smelled like the earth.

She especially loved how the rocks would feel cold at first, but then they would get hot - as they shared the heat from her body.
She felt that the rocks could feel her - like they were one together - a part of each other.

Now, Grayson loved climbing trees - And the higher the tree, the better!
He would climb high into a great big tree - And just sit up there looking at the sky – while thinking about life things.

He loved the way he felt when he was close to the sky.

With the wind blowing - And the sun shining on his face - it made him feel like he was part of the tree and the whole sky.
It was like they were one together - part of each other.

Whitney thought a lot about her inside feelings - And Grayson thought a lot about life and how things worked.

They loved talking about all kinds of things with each other - And they often shared their reeeeal inside thoughts and feelings about life - and even the upsetting stuff.

It didn't matter to them - that they sometimes thought about things differently.
They enjoyed each other anyway - because they loved learning from each other.

Whitney and Grayson really, really, reeeally - enjoyed exploring life together.
They especially liked playing in the dirt - And getting as dirty as they could.

Every day, when they took their little walking adventures - they would always stop at the strawberry field.
They would lie down in the dirt - And eat fresh strawberries right off the bush.

They loved just laying there - watching the clouds in the sky - shape into things like - birds, dogs, cats, trees, and funny faces.

And sometimes - the clouds even looked like them!

Then, they would spend the rest of their time looking for the perfect rocks for Whitney - And the best and highest treetops for Grayson.

BUT - today would be different.
Today - after lying down in the field eating strawberries - And watching the clouds form into magical shapes - Whitney and Grayson would learn about a new magical place.

They would learn about the magic that lived in the forest - And the mysteeeerious... Woodland Angels.

Aaaaand, they would also learn a lot of very wise things - about life and people and even themselves - that they didn't even know!

Today - their walk together - would lead them to the edge of the woods.
The very woods they were always told - to not ever enter alone.

JUST

WONDERING

ABOUT

LIFE

Today, the sun was shining bright - and the air was Ohhhh, so quiet.
Well, except for the birds singing
         frogs ribbiting
      crickets cricketing
         And squirrels chirping.

On this magical day - Whitney and Grayson met at the river after school - just like they always do.

Their daily adventure began with lying in the grass at the strawberry field. And, of course - munching on their after school snack - of fresh strawberries picked right from the plants.

Then, like always - they would begin searching - for the most extraordinary rocks and highest treetops.

Whitney, however - noticed that Grayson wasn't acting like his regular self.
He wasn't acting happy and excited - he was acting kind of sad and upset.

Now, Whitney has seen him feeling like this before.
She knew that sometimes, the adults in Grayson's family - were unhappy and upset with each other.

And this always made him feel sad and confused - because he just wanted everyone to be happy, kind, and loving.
Just like he and Whitney are together.

Whitney understands this, too - because she feels the same way sometimes.

When she sees her family or friends Or people on TV -
acting angry, mean, and hurtful to other people and animals... It upsets her so very much.

They just didn't understand why some people wanted to be mean and angry,
Or hurtful and upset.
They thought that if they could always be so happy, kind, and loving -
Why couldn't everyone else be that way too?

They wondered - and wondered - and wondered about this.
Whitney and Grayson often talked about the icky ways people behave - almost every day.
They thought - and wondered - and thought - and wondered -
Why in the world would anyone want to think and feel Icky?
And why would they ever - want to make other people feel Icky?!

To Whitney and Grayson, that was just totally - Whack-a-doodled!
They didn't EVER want to think Icky things - or feel yucky feelings!
For goodness' sake - It just doesn't feel good - At all!

They tried very hard not to feel bad – but sometimes it just happened.
Today, Grayson was feeling kind of blue - And Whitney just wanted him to feel better.

Grayson was walking with his head down - kicking up the dirt on the road.

So Whitney said, "Grayson, why are you not your happy little self today?
Are you thinking about upset people again?"

Grayson sighed and said, "Yeah, my family was arguing - And being mean to each other - Again!

Then, they acted upset with me, and I didn't even do anything to them!
Plus, there are kids at school who are acting mean too.
It's like - no one cares about being nice to other people!
They don't even see how unhappy - and unloving they are being.
I just don't understand."

Whitney said, "Yeah. I know what you mean.
It's like some people always want to be upset about something - Or - they are always mad at someone.
It's like they don't even want to feel good - or be good.
They don't even see how much easier it is - to just be happy and loving!"

Grayson said, "Yeh! And worse - they don't even see that they are teaching kids to be the same way!
And to make it even moooore - whack-a-doodled - kids get in trouble for saying and doing the same things they do!
It's just nuts, I tell you!"

Whitney giggled and said, "Yep. When you're right - You're right!

Maybe we won't ever understand it.
That's why I love walking outside and searching for very special rocks.
The rocks always make me feel good inside.
They make me feel like everything is going to be okay."

Grayson said, "Yes, that's why I love sitting in the treetops too.
But, Whitney - is everything going to be okay?
I mean, adults were children like us once too.
They used to be happy and loving when they were kids.
But, then they got older - And a lot of them aren't that way anymore.

Plus! - Aren't they supposed to be showing us - the best things about life -
And helping us stay a good person?
Oh, No! Whitney! Are we going to grow up to be unhappy, unloving adults too?!"

Whitney chuckled and said, "I don't know. I hope not!"

Grayson quickly said, "WELL! I think it should be the other way around!
I think the adults should remember how to be happy and loving - from kids like you and me!"

Whitney chuckled a little because - Well, he was absolutely right!

Whitney didn't really know if they would grow up - to be unhappy and unloving.
But, she did know - they had to find an answer.
And she knew she had to help Grayson feel happy again.

Because you see - since Grayson was feeling upset - she could feel it inside herself too.
His upset - was now making her feel upset too!

Now, Whitney did not like feeling unhappy at all - And she wasn't going to let herself or Grayson keep feeling that way.
So she made herself do something special - something that would make her feel good inside again.

She bent down and grabbed a beautiful rock - that way lying on the ground.
Whitney immediately noticed - that this was no ordinary rock.
This was a very special rock - because this rock... had Angel wings etched into it.

As the rock warmed in her hand - she got a strange "inside" feeling.
She didn't know why, but she just knew - deep inside herself that those wings on the rock - were a spectacular sign.

She felt that somehow - those wings would show them the answer to why people act icky.

Right then - Whitney smiled and decided to do the one thing - that would help Grayson feel better.
She said - "Come on, Grayson, let's go climb a huge tree!"

Grayson smiled because he knew what she was doing. She was trying to help him feel better - And he was so happy she cared about his feelings.

He said, "OK, OK, Whit - when you're right - you're right!
Maybe we will find the answers another day.
Come on - let's go climb an awesome tree!"

And just as they turned around - to go search for that very special huge tree to climb... they realized...

They were standing at the edge of the woods.

INTO

THE

WISE WOODS

Just then - Whitney and Grayson noticed something down by their feet.
Why! It was a group of cute little Earthworms - inching slowly across the ground!
There must have been a hundred of them!

One cute, chubby little earthworm stood up and said, "Hi, we are the Ryan's - The Ryan earthworms - that is!"

Whitney and Grayson were a little surprised the earthworms could talk!
As the army of earthworms inched by Whitney and Grayson - they all smiled and said - "Well, Hello there, kids - it's so nice to meet you!"

Grayson then asked, "Are all of you are named Ryan?"
The chubby little earthworm said, "Why, of course!"

Then, Whitney said, "But, there are like a hundred of you!
Why do all of you have the same name?"

The chubby little earthworm said - "Well, we are all made quite the same, you see - And we all think and feel the same wonderful way - so, why not!"

All of a sudden - the army of earthworms stopped inching.

The little chubby earthworm said, "Young man, will you please pick me up - so that I may talk with you?"

So - Grayson did. He picked him up very gently.

Grayson and the little chubby Ryan earthworm - looked each other - right in the eyes.

The little earthworm said, "Haven't you ever wondered why only people have separate names - but other things - like a raccoon, fireflies, and trees - are really only called one name?

A raccoon is a raccoon - A firefly is a firefly - and trees are trees.
They don't have names like Peggy or Dave, Harris, or June."

Grayson and Whitney both said at the very same time - "Why you are right! - We never thought about that!
So why don't other things have separate names like people do?"

The chubby little earthworm said, "Ahhh, curiosity! - I love it!
Those questions, dear children - are the wise things about life that the Woodland Angels will teach you!
Now, we must inch along, children."

So, Grayson gently set the chubby little earthworm back down on the ground.
And all the Ryan Earthworms began inching towards the woods.

Grayson said, "Wait, wait, Mister earthworm!
How do we find the Woodland Angels - so we can learn the wise things about life from them?"

Just then, all the earthworms stopped in their tracks.

They all turned around at the very same time - And in their tiny little wormy voices, they said - "Why children, you must enter the woods, of course!"
It is then - that the Angels - will find you!

And you sure don't want to miss what happens in these woods!
So come on in!"
Then, all the little Ryan Earthworms scooted joyfully into the forest.

Whitney looked at Grayson and said, "Ooohhh, Graaayson,
I'm feeeeling it! We need to go into the woods - because it really feels good to me - inside!"

Now, Whitney has always wanted to go into the forest.
She always felt inside of herself there was something - something very magical and special in there.

Maybe, because she figured there would be some really special rocks in the woods - And great big giant trees for Grayson to climb.

But, today - she had a deeper inside feeling.
There was something very special waiting for them.

And who knows? - maybe an adventure in the woods - would give them answers to their questions about life and people.

She did, after all, find an awesome rock with Angel wings on it!
Plus - they just met a hundred talking earthworms - telling them about Angels - And wisdom - And special things.
So it just had to be magical!

Whitney said, "Grayson, it's a sign! - it's a sign, I tell you!
It's a sign that there are great things in those woods!
And maybe we will even meet real live Angels too!"

Grayson knew that Whitney reeeaaally wanted to go into the woods - because she always does.
Normally, Grayson always talks her out of it. But - today is different.

They were older now - And - they were together.
But, most importantly, they had some pretty important life questions they wanted to find answers to.
Plus, how bad could it the woods really be?!

Whitney said, "Graaayson - come on, come on, pleeeease, let's go in!"

Grayson stood there at the edge of the woods, thinking for a moment.
Then he said, "Okay, Whit - let's do it! - let's go into the woods!"

Whitney was so excited - and filled with so much joy.
She yelled out loud - "I knew today was special! - I just knew it!
It's going to be a very special day for you too, Grayson.
You just watch and see!"

So they grabbed each other by the hand and slowly stepped into the woods.
They were both a little afraid - but only because it was a new experience for them.

They didn't really know what lived in the woods - but - they were too excited and curious to turn around.

As they looked inside the woods - it was veeeery dark and veeeery quiet.
The sun wasn't shining inside, at all,
because there were so many huge trees blocking the light.

As they stepped into the woods - a bit further -
And a little bit farther - And a little bit farther -
the darker - and quieter - and creepier - it became.

Whitney and Grayson began to hear some very strange sounds - moving through the forest.
Sounds they had never heard before.
These sounds are not like the sounds they've heard in the out-world.

These sounds are exciting and beautiful - and magical and mysterious.
So they stop walking - And their bodies froze in place.
Quietly, they listened.

Then the sounds began to get louder and louder.
And they heard weird sounds flying through the air.

One sound was so loud - and mysterious, it echoed through the forest like a huuuuge explosion.
It scared Whitney and Grayson soooo much - that they closed their eyes tight and hugged each other.

Then - after a few moments of scaredy-cat hugging - they opened their eyes and held each other's hand tightly.

They turned around to see what the sound was.
The woods were so very, very dark, and they couldn't see anything.
They could only feel their hands shaking.
Then - they saw something begin to glow in the woods.

They saw tiny, glowing dots - fluttering all around - in, and out - up and down – and through the trees.
Now, these little dots weren't scary at all.
They were quite magical!

Plus, those glowing dots were all giggling! And as they flew by, Whitney and Grayson, they were speeding around - as fast - as fast could be.
And flashing their little lights - giggling all the way.
Fluttering back and forth - And up and down - And circling every tree - round and round!

Whitney and Grayson couldn't help themselves. They began giggling too.
Now, they didn't know what those happy little dots were - But they sure were fun to watch!

Then, after a few moments – even more, sounds filled the air.
And then, strange dark shadows began to appear.

THE SHADOW DANCERS

The strange dark shadows began to dance around on the ground.
And every time Whitney and Grayson looked at a shadow dancing,
The shadows would change their appearance into them!
It was like looking at a copy of themselves!

Then, a very laaarge, dark, shadowy thing - flew very fast towards Whitney and Grayson.
It scared them so much that they both closed their eyes - And hid their faces in their hands.

Grayson said, "Ohhhh, My! Whitney let's go home! We shouldn't be in here alone!"
Just then - the large dark shadow thing swirled around them - And said, "Why lovely children, you are definitely not alone!

Today, you will experience many mysterious things - and learn secrets about life and yourselves.
And it is we, the Shadows - Who come to share the first mystery with you."

Whitney said, "But Shadow, you scared us!"
Just then - all the shadows in the woods began to giggle loudly.

The very large shadow said, "Why dear children, weeee didn't scare you!
Yooouuu - scared yourselves!
Let us help you understand this mystery!

You have given us a scary name - "The Shadows."

But - we are not actually scary, because we come from you!
We are only YOUR shadows - The part of You that is scared and afraid of things.
Shadows come from YOUR own scary thoughts and upsets.

Don't you notice that shadows only appear - when you are worried or scared?
It is not good for you to worry or be afraid.

So, when you see shadows dancing around - remember that we can help you - be your stronger self.
Just look for the real truth - instead of fear."

Grayson and Whitney understood exactly what the shadows were telling them - that was if they looked for the truth with good thoughts - instead of thinking scary things - then they wouldn't be afraid at all!

Whitney and Grayson realized now - they didn't need to be afraid of their shadows -
And they definitely didn't ever need to make scary stuff up in their head.
They just needed to be smart and learn the truth - beefooore, they get themselves all scared up!"

Whitney and Grayson laughed at themselves.
Grayson said - "How silly are we?!
We're being all afraid when we don't even know what the truth is.

I am soooo - being brave with good thoughts from now on!
And I'm always going to look for the truth - beeefooore I make stuff up in my head!"

Then, the very large shadow said - "Let me help you understand more about the truth.
The truth to anything is what you know to be real and true inside of yourself.

It is not always what your brain thinks or fears.
It's only your inside feelings - that are good and real.

A lot of what other people say can be untrue, too, because - when people feel bad about themselves - they sometimes make stories up - or change the truth.

So when people say hurtful things about you – You know inside that it isn't true – So, don't believe it.
They might be making up stories - just to help them feel better about themselves.

Like, if someone says nasty things about how you look - like calling you fat or ugly - Or a dummy or a mommy's boy.
Or - if they say you have a big nose or funny ears - Or – if they say you dress funny or are poor.

None of those things are EVER - the truth - because everyone is perfect - just the way they are!
The truth there is - They are probably just making stuff up - because they are afraid to be their real, good self.

Another truth is that your outer body - is just a home for your inside person.
Everyone's body is made differently - And for a very special reason.

Your body protects your inside person - And that inside person teaches you to be happy with your beauty - And being different.
And, most important of all - your inside self loves you - just the way you are.

You are not ever what anyone says you are. You can always believe you are wonderful, just the way you were made!
Because you Are!... And THAT is the truth!"

Whitney and Grayson began to remember - what some people have said about them that was untrue.
As they listened and understood the Shadows' message - they began to feel very happy and brave inside.

Grayson said, "Wow! The Shadows are right!
We don't have to be afraid to love ourselves - And we should, inside and out!

I can't wait to tell people who feel bad about themselves - that they are wonderful - just the way they are!"

Then - when the shadows heard Whitney and Grayson understand - they all - just magically disappeared.

And then, A shining ray of sunlight beamed brightly into the forest.

Whitney and Grayson were now definitely - feeling the wisdom - And magic - and mystery - the little earthworms told them about.

Just then - Whitney felt something touch her arm. And whatever it was - let out a joyful little giggle.

So she turned around to see what it was. And all she saw was a misty golden light swirling around her.

Then, it sped off through the woods - twisting and turning - leaving a long stream of light - floating in the air behind it.

They watched the golden light fly around and fill the forest with joy and laughter.

Then, all of a sudden - everything became so very, very quiet again.

Whitney and Grayson just stood there in silence - curiously waiting to see what would happen next.

FOREST

LIGHTS

Then, Whitney felt something touch her - Again!
She couldn't see what it was - but she could feeeel it - spinning around her very fast.

It was making hundreds of circles around her body - like it was wrapping her up - in a warm, comfortable blanket.
So, Whitney closed her eyes - so that she could really feel - the comfort move inside her.

Then, she opened her eyes - and her mouth fell wide open.
She saw such a fantastic sight!
The entire forest was filled with a bright golden glow - And she noticed - A tube of light - swirling, slowly, through the forest.

It looked just like a beautiful, dancing ballerina.
The kind of ballerina that dances with long ribbons.

After watching the beautiful dance for a moment - Whitney realized that Grayson wasn't next to her anymore.
She looked around and called out - "Grayson, where are you?"

Grayson said, "Whit, I'm right here."
He was sitting on the ground next to her - holding a rock in the palm of his hand.
He said, "Woah, Whitney, look, this is a magic rock - it has lights inside of it!"

Whitney bent down, looked at the rock, and said, "Wow, it does!

That's soooo cool. I wonder what those lights are?!"
Then - gently, one by one - The little lights began to float out of the rock.
And when they did - each light twisted into a swirling tube of light.
All those little swirling tubes of light were gliding through the air.

Then, one tube of light swirled around - And went right into another tube of light. And it got bigger!
Then, each and every tube of light - began twirling around each other.

Then they all spiraled together - And made themselves into one tube!
And it got bigger, and bigger, and bigger. It was huge!

Finally, after the last light entered the one huge tube - It blew up like a firework!
And when it exploded - a thousand glowing ladybugs shot out into the air.
My goodness! - there were little glowing ladybugs everywhere!

They had little flashing lights, too - just like fireflies do.
There were thousands of them flying all around - Lighting and flashing.
They were all dancing together, in the air - And giggling - like they just didn't care!

Now, since feelings make other people and animals feel the same-
Whitney and Grayson couldn't help themselves - they started dancing and giggling together too!

Then - one of the flashing ladybugs - with her tiny little ladybug voice - flew right up to Whitney and Grayson and said…

"Hi, there! We are the Makaiya Ladybugs!
And we have come to tell you another life mystery."

Then, all the Makaiya ladybugs said together, at the same time -
"Always remember - it is the joy you feel inside yourself - that gives you light and makes you feel happy.

And it is the light inside of you - that makes you dance and shine your most special self.
Just like us, now - sharing our light and happiness with you.
You, too - are to dance happily and share your light with others.

Whitney and Grayson's eyes stretched wide open. All they could say was -
"Wow - Wow - Wow!"
Because - after hearing the Makaiya ladybug's secret message - they knew they were definitely learning very special, important things about life - And themselves.

Grayson said - "Makaiya Ladybug - does that mean when we don't feel happy or feel like dancing - that the light of joy is not inside of us?"

All the Makaiya ladybugs, all together, said - "Darlings, it means - when you don't feel like dancing and laughing - then you must go do something happy and joyful - to make yourself dance and laugh!

You must make an effort to do things that make you feel joyful.
And then, share your joy with others - so they can learn how to do it too."

Now, Grayson, being a deep thinker, understood this message clearly.
At first, he was feeling upset - and even a little scared.

But when he saw the ladybug lights dancing and laughing - he automatically felt their joy.
He began to feel the exact same way - and he definitely felt better!

The ladybugs taught him to dance and laugh - And to shine his feelings with joy - And he felt okay to just be himself.

He knew for sure now - that he would find all of his answers in these woods - And maybe even a lot more life secrets, he never even knew.

And Whitney, being a deep feeler - also understood this secret.
That is exactly what she did for Grayson earlier when he was upset.

She made an effort - to go do something that would bring him joy - by suggesting they go climb a tree!

Whitney, like Grayson - was feeling very perfect - And quite magical inside of herself.
The two of them were sooo very excited - And they were reeeally enjoying all the wisdom their new forest friends were sharing with them!

Just then, all the Makaiya ladybugs gathered together - into one huge tremendous swarm.

And they all spoke together - at the same time, and said - "That's all you and life are really about, dear ones - sharing your good self."

Then, the huge swarm flew over to a very large - very old, ancient tree in the middle of the woods.

Grayson could tell it was a very old tree - because of the lines and shape of the bark.
He knew about these life things, you know.

Whitney could tell that it was a very wise old tree too - because she could feeeel its energy.
She knew about feeling things, you know.

As they were standing there together looking and feeling the tree - they saw the Makaiya ladybug swarm - And they began circling around the old tree.
Round and round the tree, they went.

The swarm was flying so fast - that they started to go invisible.
All Whitney and Grayson could see now - was just tiny lines - streaking through the air.

Then, all of a sudden - out of nowhere - A ginoooormous bright, purple light - lit up the entire forest.
It was so brilliant - that it blinded Whitney and Grayson for a few moments!

And then ~ when their eyesight returned - what do you think they saw?!

THE WOODS

COME ALIVE

They saw...
   Little fairies with starlit wings - flying all around.
    Little white bunnies wearing halos - hopping up and down.
     Little yellow flowers - singing a soft, lovely melody.
      And an army of glow-worms with hats - marching across the ground.

And every one of these magical lives - were all saying - "Helloooo"
And in all different kinds of cute, little critter voices.

Whitney and Grayson heard greetings from...
   Joyful little fairy voices
    Heavenly little bunny voices
     Whispering little glow-worm voices
      And loving musical flower voices

Then - all the tiny fairies with starlit wings - flew up to Whitney and Grayson and said - in their tiny fairy voices - "Hellooo, lovelies!
It's so very nice to meet you! - Our name is Jessica.

And like the Earthworms and everyone in the woods - we are all named the same.
We all have the same name too - because – Inside - we are all made the same!

Our bodies are put together the same way - And we all have the same bones, organs, and Spirit.

We all need the same things to live - And we all need food, water, and air to breathe - And, of course, lots of love!

We all have the same brain with good smarts inside too.
And we were all happy and joyful from the very day that we were born.

So you see - to separate ourselves from each other - with names and words - would be quite silly!"

Then, all the little white bunnies wearing halo's - hopped over and said - in their fuzzy, little bunny voices -
"Hellooo, there! It's so nice to meet you! - Our name is Brooklyn,

And we, too, are all named the same - because we are all the same.
Like everyone else - We all need food, water, and air to breathe - And, of course, lots of love!

We all have love and gentleness inside, too - since the very day we were born.
Plus, we all hop around the same - Aaannd, we all have the same beautiful halo!

So you see - to separate ourselves from each other - with names and words - would be quite silly!"

Then, all the pretty little singing yellow flowers popped up.
Standing up very high and tall - And in their soft, little flower voices - they all said - "Hellooo, there - It's so nice to meet you! Our name is Payton,

And we, too, are all named the same because - well, we are just all the same!

We are all pretty, soft, and delicate - And we need light, good energy, and a place to grow strong.
And we all need the same things to live - food, water, and air to breathe - And, of course, lots of love!
So you see - to separate ourselves from each other - with names and words would be quite silly."

Then, the cutest little glow-worms that you ever did see - marched over and took off their tiny glow-worm hats.

They said - in their tiny little glow-worm voices - "Hellooo, children! It's so nice to meet you!
Our name is Jacob, and we are all named the same - because we too - need the same things to live - food, water, light, and air to breath - And lots of love!

Aaaand - we all have gentle togetherness - so we can work together as a helpful team.
Plus, when we all join together - we can shine our great light into dark places - so that everyone can see - and find their way.

And we all know the same thing too. We know that is the way we are supposed to stay - just as we were the very day we were born.

And children - Everything the fairies, bunnies, flowers, and us need - You do too!
So you see - to separate yourselves from each other - with names and words - would be quite silly!"

Right then, Whitney and Grayson realized that everyone – no matter if it was people, animals, plants, or insects - every living thing - needs the same things to live.
And every living thing - is really made the same way, inside.
And even though things look different on the outside - everything needs love.

Whitney and Grayson understood that when people call people names - they separate them from knowing togetherness.
They knew too - that using words to separate things - can make things appear untrue.

Whitney and Grayson realized in a flash of a moment that togetherness - And who they are inside - is more important than names and words.
Because that is how they were made - from the very day they were born!

Then, the Jessica fairies said - "Let us share another mystery with you...
People are given separate names - Not because you are different inside.

You are given separate names - so that other people can keep track - of "who is who" in the world!
It's just a way to tell who is who - by their outside self.
But that doesn't mean the inside self - is the same."

Then, all the glow-worms spoke up and said - "Soooo - if you are ever called names - Or you feel separated or alone... just use your inside brain smarts!

Only remember what is true - inside of YOU.
All things are born, needing the same things to live.

Everything needs food - and water - and air to breathe - And everything needs good wisdom.

Everything needs happiness, love, and gentleness - And everything is pretty. Everything is delicate - And everything has a beautiful voice inside - And everyone needs togetherness, good energy, and space to grow.

All these things together are what makes everything and everyone - shine their happy light.
And when these things are shining brightly inside of you - everyone feels love.

And when your light shines - It helps others see their inside self - so that they can find their way too.
That's just how all things are made - from the very day they were born!"

Grayson, with his head down, then said - "Since we are all born - with the same things and needs - then why do some people grow up to be unhappy, unloving - And separated from each other?"

Then, all the little Brooklyn bunnies shouted out - "Oh, Oh, we know, we know why!
Then, they said - "People grow up to be unhappy, unloving, and separated from each other - because they forget how to be the way they were born.
They forget everyone, and everything is made to work together.

Because people, nature, animals, and plants live together!
So you see, without togetherness – it's quite hard for people to stay happy and loving.

Now, people may talk about togetherness - but that doesn't make them feeeel or act with togetherness.

Togetherness, like all good stuff - can only be felt inside - when we think and do things with happiness and love."

Whitney said, "Oh, yes, like Grayson and me!
We have happiness, love, AND togetherness - just like we did when we were born - Right?"

The little yellow Payton flowers all together - began to sing a pretty little melody.
They sang -
"Oh, Yes! Oh, Yes! - Little one - That is so very true!
You have happiness, love, and togetherness - all over - inside and out of you.
And everywhere, through and through!"

Grayson said - "Oh, I am so glad that we do!
Because I have seen people without happiness, love, and togetherness - And it doesn't feel good to me inside - At All!"

Just then, all the Jacob glow-worms began glowing very brightly.
They said... "Whitney and Grayson - we shine our light for you - so that you may see your way.

Now, turn around - And let the magic of the wise, old, ancient tree - take you awaaaaaay."

Whitney and Grayson and all the critters turned around.
They all stood silent - And watched the old tree.

Then - they saw the old, ancient tree begin to move - And sparkling lights flickered inside the tree.
It began to grow bigger, and bigger, and bigger.

Its limbs began stretching and twisting outward - all throoough the woods - Far and wide - and longer and longer.

Well, now, Grayson began to feel a little nervous.
He said, in a scaredy-cat tone, "Ummm, Whitney - that tree is growing awwwwful big!"

Whitney said, "Yep, it sure is! - It's so cool, isn't it?! - I wonder what it's going to do?!"

Grayson said - in a soft, whispering, shaky voice - "Ummmm, I'm trying not to be afraid - like the shadows taught us...
Buuuut - That tree isn't like a wicked tree of the forest - Is it?
It isn't going to come grab us up with its limbs - Is it?"

Whitney giggled and said, "Oh No - No way, Grayson!
Nothing that magical and beautiful - would ever harm us!"

And then, just as she finished saying that - the entire forest went dark.
And all the magical sounds in the forest just stopped.

There were no more lights.

No more Makaiya ladybugs - And no more Jessica fairies.

No more Brooklyn bunnies - And no more singing Payton flowers.
And no more Jacob glow-worms.

Only silence filled the woods - And complete blackness surrounded Grayson and Whitney.

WISHES

AND

MYSTERIES

Now, Whitney and Grayson began to feel a little afraid again - being surrounded by all that silent darkness.
But, they made themselves remember what the shadows said.

The shadows said - "They were not to worry - Or make things up in their head, until they knew the real truth."

And even though - a tiny part of them was scared - They stayed strong - because inside, they knew... the truth would appear.
Plus, they both felt inside - something extraordinary was about to happen.

They knew that something amazing was going on here.
So, at that very moment - Grayson made a prayer inside, quietly, in his head...

"He wished that everyone - all the people in the world - would choose to be happy and loving to themselves - And every living thing.
So then they could feel the magic like he and Whitney are.

Then, just as he said his prayer...
   Every light -
    Every tree -
     Every animal -
      and Every magical sound - heard his wish too.
       And the woods came alive!
        The entire forest - was full of lights, love, and happy energy again!

So you see - Grayson's hope for people - made the darkness go away.
Then the light could shine again - inside of him - and everywhere.

Well, Grayson was very amazed at himself.
He was quite proud, too - because he didn't let his scary thoughts make him upset.

Then, the group of Ryan earthworms inched by - And they all said together, at the very same time - "Helloo, again, friends!
We are so glad you are enjoying the woods!

We welcome you to enjoy all of our wisdom, happiness, and love!
Now, we will share with you - another mystery of life -
So that you may reeaaaly understand your wonderful prayer, Grayson!

Grayson said, But, but How do you know my prayer?
I said it in my head, not out loud?!

The Earthworms said… "Oh! That mystery is not the one to know… Yet!
The mystery to know Is - before anyone can really and truly be happy and loving - They must be kind and loving to themselves, first!"

Grayson didn't even have time to think anymore - About how the earthworms knew about the prayer he said in his head.
Because - right then, A beautiful flock of white doves flew in - And perched upon a tree branch.

They all said together, at the very same time - "Helloooo, children. Our name is Rylee - And we have a mystery to share with you too!

The mystery we would like you to know is - you must always be kind to yourselves - both inside and out.
And that will require you to work hard - at having good, kind thoughts about others inside your head!"

Then - A swarm of honey bees buzzed in.
And they all hovered - right in front of Whitney and Grayson.
They all said together, at the very same time - "Buzz, Buzz, Greetings, kids! Our name is Jonah - And we have a mystery to share with you, too.

This mystery to know is that - in life, you must fly high above troubles - just like we do!

Remember not to let what other people say or do - sting your feelings!
What others think, say, and do comes from their own brain.
And since their brain is not your brain - nothing is ever true - until you believe it's true."

Just then, all the shadows and glowing mists
 And all the fairies named Jessica
   And all the bunnies named Brooklyn
     And all the ladybugs named Makaiya
       And all the glow-worms named Jacob
         And all the yellow flowers named Payton
           All joined together and yelled out with such joy
             "Whitney and Grayson, we welcome you - And we love you!"

At that moment - all the critters in the woods - began to laugh and giggle.
They all started dancing around the forest - doing the "Chicken Dance."

All their happiness, love, and joy, Of course - got all over Whitney and Grayson - inside and out.
So they began doing the Chicken Dance too!

And as they laughed - danced - and clucked - And flapped their wing-like arms in the air.
The happiest, joyful energy they had ever felt - echoed throughout the entire forest!

All the laughter and good, happy energy spread out far and wide - touching and filling up every animal - And every space in the woods.

What do you think happened to everything in the woods, then?
Well, Everything felt happy and joyful too!

The ground was vibrating, and trees were swaying.
   Birds were dancing, and rocks were shining.
     Even the shadows began to brighten!

Whitney and Grayson were filled up with so much love and togetherness.
Their bodies inside felt like a huge shining bright light!

Now, they truly knew - what being happy and loving to yourself inside and out - really means.

They had never had so much fun - being happy, silly - And loving with themselves!

Then just as everyone was having a blast dancing - clucking - laughing...
And flapping around like happy, little chicken birds.

There came a new, very BIIIIG sound - moving through the forest.

A

FOREST

MONSTER?

HA!

This big sound was coming out of the large, old, ancient tree!
It sounded like a huge old creaky door opening - Creeeaaak

Whatever it was, it sounded very large - And very strong - And - Oh, so mighty and powerful!

Whitney and Grayson then noticed that all the critters in the woods - immediately laid down on the ground - in silence.
They were all waiting - for that huge, mighty thing to appear.

Then, the ground began to shake - like an earthquake.
The trees shook and moved from side to side - And all the forest critters were holding on tight.

Grayson whispered quietly to Whitney - "Oh, No, Whitney!
What if it's a forest monster!? - What if it's a forest monster?!"

But - Whitney was mesmerized, and she couldn't speak!
Whitney and Grayson tried to be brave - but they were pretty scared now.
And why were they scared?
Because they made up in their heads - that whatever was coming -
was a giant, huge, scary forest monster!

Hmmm, I wonder why they didn't wait to find out the truth?
They instead - just went and got themselves all scared up - Again!

Whitney and Grayson stood very, very still - And grasped each other's hand tightly.
They held their breath - And didn't move a muscle.

They could "feel" something was watching them - from inside the ancient tree.
And they knew that whatever it was - It was definitely going to come out!

Just then, a strong wind blew through the woods.
And the leaves that were lying on the ground - lifted up into the air and swirled around like a monster tornado.

Whitney and Grayson were totally expecting - to see a huuuuge scary forest monster appear!
But instead, to their surprise, they heard a tiny, little voice giggling!

Whitney said, "Well, My, My - that doesn't sound like a forest monster at all! My goodness! - It sounds like a happy little child, giggling."

Grayson said, "Well, maybe it's a very laaarge - child forest monster!
Or - maybe it's a monster-sized leprechaun!
Or - maybe it's just a monster who has a tiny little girl voice!"

Whitney and Grayson were confused - but of course, curious.
So, they squinted their eyes really, really, tight and small - to try and see what it was - but they couldn't see much.

Then, they saw the roots and trunk of the old, ancient tree - begin to glow with the most beautiful green and white light.

It was purely magical!
The green - was as green as emeralds - And the white - was sparkling white like snow.

The glowing green and white lights - grew bigger and bigger - And its light got brighter and brighter.
But then they noticed - the light would get dimmer - And then it would get brighter again.

And then dimmer - And brighter.
They realized the old ancient tree was actually - breathing! Light!

Then, the glowing green light sparkled - like bright twinkling stars - And it began to spread up from the roots of the tree...
Through the trunk - And out into the branches - And into all the leaves.

The whole tree looked like it had a quadrillion tiny lights inside of it - Sparkling - And twinkling - And shimmering.
Whitney and Grayson had not ever seen anything like it before.

Whitney then noticed that the lights twinkling inside the tree - were not just twinkling - They were actually flying around inside the tree!
So she stepped closer to have a better look.

Grayson, chickenly said - "No, Whitney, the forest monster might get you."
But Whitney wasn't really all that afraid now.
She got right up in front of the old tree — And when she did - the tree began to shake!

Well, Whitney was startled and screamed! - And Grayson almost passed out. Haha!

Whitney said with amazement - "WOW, what a fantastic sight!
Grayson, those lights inside the tree are the Makaiya ladybugs!"

She began laughing and said, "Well, goodness gracious - we did it again! - we got all scared and upset again, over nothing!
I see the truth now - This is magical - and beautiful - And not scary at all!"

Grayson giggled shyly - because he was a little embarrassed.
Being the thinker, Grayson, naturally, was already wondering - how all the Makaiya ladybugs got to be inside the old, ancient tree.
He could only figure - it was totally magic!

And Whitney, being the feeler - wondered how awesome it must feeeel - to be flying around inside the old, ancient tree.
She could only figure that it had to feel magical.

Just then - The old ancient tree began breathing heavier.
Its trunk - moved in and out… in and out…
And then - it breathed even deeeeper… Innnnnnn - and Ouuuuuuut.

The old tree and the lights inside were expanding so far and wide - that Whitney and Grayson thought the tree would burst open!

Then another magical thing happened.

Whitney and Grayson realized - they were so amazed by the mysteries in the woods - they had completely forgotten all about their upsets.

All they cared about now - was enjoying the magic and mystery - And learning about all the little Woodland Angels.

Whitney and Grayson were thinking the very same thing - at the very same time.
They thought about how much they have learned from their new friends.
And how paying attention - to only the truth and mystery of things - is so much better than being a scaredy-cat and feeling upset!

Suddenly, their thoughts stopped when they began to hear - a majestic voice whispering from around the ancient tree.
The whisper became louder and louder - And it echoed throughout the woods.

The whispering voice said - "Dear sweet children - I have yet another life mystery for you to know.
The Woodland Angels hope you will understand - that when you pay attention to only the good and magical things… it will always make everything better - And make you feel better!"

Whitney and Grayson's eyes bugged-out wide with such curiosity.
The beautiful, mysterious voice whispered again, saying -
"If you are always scared and worried - you won't be able to recognize good, magical things.

That is just how your brain works! - when you focus on anything - your brain will always give you more of what you are thinking about!

So make what you think, feel, and believe - Great and mysterious.
Then - your brain will give you more good stuff to understand!

And know too, you will need to be strong and brave enough - to focus on good things - because other people may want you to think in not-so-good ways.

Just remember, their ways - are their ways - And it doesn't ever have to be your way.

THE MAGICAL WOMAN

OF

THE FOREST

Whitney and Grayson, at the very same time - called out to the whispering voice.
They said - "Um, excuse me... hello, beautiful voice - who are you?
Oh, won't you please come out so that we may meet you?"

Just then - they saw a bright, emerald green light - slowly streaming out of the old, ancient tree.
This bright green light - spiraled out - a thick stream of swirling green smoke.

And it began floating towards Whitney and Grayson.
Then, it twisted - and twirled - in all kinds of directions.

Whitney and Grayson knew it was going to shape into something - And they wondered what in the world could it be?

Then, the green glowing smoke began to fade away - And as it did - there stood a beautiful green Woman.
She sparkled - like a million emeralds in the sunlight.

She had hundreds of colorful wings - gently waving behind her - And they changed into many different colors - like a kaleidoscope.

Whitney and Grayson noticed, too - she had a glittery golden light that trailed behind her as she walked toward them.
And every time the Magical Woman took a step - her wings giggled.

And - her footprints on the ground - left a glittery, green footprint wherever she walked!

The closer the green Woman came to them - the more magnificent they felt inside.

Just watching her, they felt so comfortable and loved.

It was as if her love was inside of them - all together with them.

Just like when Whitney feels like the rocks are part of her - And when Grayson feels like the trees and sky are part of him.

Whitney and Grayson could see the glittering green glowing Woman now - she was fully visible - As she stood before them.

Her colorful wings were blowing gently behind her - And she is holding the cutest little puppy - cradled gently in her arms.

The magical glowing Woman giggled and said, "Here I am, Sweet Angels!

I am The Magical Woman of the Forest - And this is my darling little Angel puppy - Doodlekobi.

We walk close to Earth together - And share the good wisdom of all the Nature Spirits.

We also help the Angels share their messages to people - And all living things - here and beyond.

I have come to share very special Angel messages about life with you.

I can help you understand wise, beautiful things about yourselves - so you may grow with love - And know how to live beyond things that upset you."

Whitney and Grayson's mouth were wide open, gazing at her as she spoke.
Then, at the very same time, they said... "Oh, thank you, Magical Woman, of the Forest - but what upsets would that be?"

Just then, every creature in the forest - busted out laughing - And a family of raccoons, all named Allison - fell over on their backs - rolling back and forth - laughing out loud!

They were all laughing because Whitney and Grayson, Again - had completely forgotten that they were ever upset!

There was a cute little family of foxes, all named Emily - who were laughing hysterically too - because they knew Whitney and Grayson had just learned another great mystery - And they didn't even know it.

Whitney started laughing, too - because laughter is contagious.
But she was confused so looked to the Magical Woman and said - "Magical Woman, why is everyone laughing?"

The Magical Woman giggled too and said - "Well, it's because you are soooo happy - And have forgotten all about what you were upset about when you entered these woods.

See, that is how upsets magically disappear - when you are happy and laughing! Now, isn't that amazing?!
Laughter IS the best medicine for any upset you ever have!"

Whitney said, "Oh, My! What wonderful wisdom that is Magical Woman!"

The Magical Woman then said, Oh dear one's, how to get rid of upsets - is no longer a mystery to you.
You now know that enjoying your natural, happy self - is your nature - And it is the key to all things good.

When you fill your mind with natural things - And focus on the happy, beautiful things in life - just as you are right now - upsetting things won't feel so bad anymore."

The magical women of the forest then said, "Lovely children - do you remember, before coming into the woods - when you were thinking about unhappy, unkind people?

Then, once you decided to do something different - And entered the woods - You didn't even think about unhappy, unkind people anymore - And your upsets didn't matter.

See, that is because you "chose" to do something better - And more fun and interesting.
Plus, meeting all of your new friends in the woods - Helped you change your focus to having fun - so see, good friends can help too!"

Whitney and Grayson said, "Yes! Yes! - It IS magic! - we aren't upset anymore at all!
We haven't thought about yucky stuff the whole time - ever since we entered the woods!"

The Magical Woman said, "Exactly! That's because when you are surrounded with happy, beautiful things - you automatically busy your mind with the good stuff - And your thoughts magically change for the better.

It's magic, I tell you! And, that magic is inside of you - And every living thing - at all times.
Everyone can choose to think about good things - And, good thoughts will always fix upsets.

When you are having upset, sadness, fear, or anger - Or even when you are feeling icky with a cold or a bellyache - if you want to feel better – then busy yourself with things that make you feel good and happy inside.
Just laugh yourself better!"

The Magical Woman then said - "My darling children - you must not forget that people's upsets are - After all - their own.
And it is not healthy for you - to make their upsets - your upsets.

Grayson yelled out joyfully - "Oh, Yes! - I knew the forest would have an answer for me!
That is exactly why some adults are not happy and loving - like they were when they were born - isn't it?!
They are choosing to focus on things that make them feel icky - instead of laughing and making happy choices for themselves!"

Grayson said, "Oh, Magical Woman - thank you so much for helping us understand!"

Then, he said - "Ummm, Magical Woman - can we bring all the unhappy and unloving people here to these woods - so they can learn this secret too?!"

The Magical Woman giggled and said, "My sweets - there, in your question - is yet another great life mystery.
You see, the Woodland Angels have helped you understand many things - So that you may teach others when you leave the woods.

When you share knowledge with others - you must remember - that each person must first want - to be good, happy, and feel the beauty inside of themselves.
They must want to feel the magic of life - And how special they are.

You cannot force anyone to do anything - because everyone has their own magical way to live life - And for great and wise reasons too.

And my darlings - the easiest way to help others is to be the example of the wisdom you have learned here today.
Then, everyone will see your happiness - And naturally - they will want to feel the better part of themselves.

Just as the glow-worms and Whitney set the example for you - to want to enter the forest.
You wanted to find answers to your upset questions - And you wanted to feel better.

So, the glow-worms showed up all happy - And Whitney helped changed your focus when she suggested that you enter the woods!
See - it's just that easy to be a good example!"

Grayson said, "Oh, yes, we did! - And boy, Ohhhh boy - I definitely do feel good and happy inside again!
And we are most definitely getting so many wise answers - to our questions about life, people, and ourselves!"

The Magical Woman of the Forest said, "Now, children, you must also know that you have great power to help people with your knowledge.
When you share your wisdom with others - you must remember that your wisdom is yours - And their wisdom is theirs.

But - the real wisdom happens when you put two wisdoms together! - And, that is when learning is most powerful.

Whitney and Grayson said together - the very same thing.
They said, "Oh, Magical Woman, we will! - we will absolutely remember everything - And, we will be the example - And, we will share what we've learned with others to help them learn their own power too!"

The Magical Woman then said, "Lovely children - I have been watching you - for quite some time now.
I have been waiting for you to be brave enough - to trust your inside selves.

Aren't you glad you entered the woods?!
If you had not wanted to search for better wisdom - you would not have met all of us in these wise, old woods - And you wouldn't have enjoyed exploring the magical happiness of your inside selves.

I thank you for your bravery and for sharing yourselves with us all.
Now, would you like to meet more friends in the forest?
Are you ready to experience even more mysteries about yourselves?"

Whitney and Grayson smiled and looked at each other like - Um, silly question! Excitedly, of course, they said – "Oh, Yes! - Oh, Yes! - Please, please, show us more!"

Grayson then said, "Magical Woman, we've heard there are Angels in the woods - are we going to meet real live Angels?"

The Magical Woman giggled and said, "Why yes! Yes, you will!
But only when the light shines inside of you - And you realize that you are dear Angels yourselves.

This must happen because the real live Angels in these woods - have very powerful energy - So you must first be prepared with great wisdom - so you will be able to understand their life messages.

Angel wisdom helps everyone grow spiritually - And helps All living things grow to be faithful, strong, wise, loving adults.

That is why I stand before you.
It is my position to help you understand - the great, loving, Angel wisdom that is inside of you."

A

new

WORLD

At that very moment - a million butterflies fluttered by - And they all said together, in a million little butterfly voices - "Hello, children! Our name is Aaliyah - And we have a life mystery to share with you too!

Always remember to choose how you want to feel.
Only you feel what's inside of you - No one else can.

So that gives you all the power to choose what you want to feel.
No one can make you feel anything - that you don't want to feel!

So, if you don't like feeling mad - then don't think you are mad!
If you don't like feeling sad - then don't believe you are sad!
And, if you like feeling happy - then know you are happy!
And, if you want to feel love - then feel love!"

Now, Grayson's mouth is wide open with amazement - yet, again.
He then said, "Oh, beautiful Aaliyah butterflies - you are so right!

I remember one day at school - a friend told me that I should be mad at another friend - all because my friend forgot to do something.

I said I wasn't going to be mad at him for forgetting - we all do that. But inside of me - I didn't want to be mad because I didn't want to feel the feelings of being upset.

Is that what the mystery is about?"
The Aaliyah butterflies all giggled with joy and said, "Why yes! Yes, Grayson! - that is the perfect example!

And, let us tell you too - We are so very proud of you - for keeping good thoughts in your mind. And that is what keeps your feelings and body well!

You see, when YOU choose to stay with good thoughts and feelings - you are being very wise and good to yourself!
But, when you choose to be upset and unhappy - that spreads out and brings upset and unhappiness to others.
Even your pets feel it! - And, even plants feel it!

So making sure you choose what you really want to feel helps you - but it also helps all other living things.

Plus, making good feeling choices for yourself makes you strong and wise enough - to be able to say NO to things that just don't feel right inside of you.
- And to keep you well and safe - You will probably need to say No, to a lot of things in life."

Grayson smiled a little sideways grin - And began singing a little song as he danced around - He sang - "Yeah, Yeah, I'm wise - And I feel good -
I choose to be happy and strong - Yeah, Yeah,
because I can - Yeah Yeah,
And, this is my song!"

All the Aaliyah butterflies giggled and said - "Why, of course, you are strong and wise - everyone is!"

The butterflies then said, "Children, just do what your own good wisdom tells you - instead of doing things that don't feel right inside of you - And your life will be magical!"

The Magical Woman thanked the Aaliyah butterflies for sharing their life mystery - And then, they all said, "You are most welcome!

And remember this too - Whenever you see a butterfly - know that it's us - reminding you to do what's good and right inside of you."
Then, all the beautiful Aaliyah butterflies fluttered off into the forest - And disappeared.

The Magical Woman said, "Whitney and Grayson, what I am going to share with you next - is a most important, magical life mystery.
As you know - people learn from each other.

People teach other people - And they even teach their pets and plants too!
But – you don't teach by just being smart.
You teach others and all living things - by your energy - And the way you feel, think and behave.

Energy is like an invisible cloud coming out of your body - And it can be a bright, beautiful cloud - Or it can be a dark and gloomy cloud.
And it all depends on what you are thinking and feeling inside of yourself.

Your body's energy cloud - is much like a light bulb putting off heat.
You can't see the heat around the light bulb, right?!
But, you can feeeel the heat if you put your hand near it.
And, if you touch it, it will burn you.

Your invisible energy cloud can do the same thing.
It can make other living things - feel good, warm, and soothing inside.
Or, it can make them feel not-so-good and hot inside.

Other people's energy can also do the same to you.
All living things - feeeel your energy - even the animals and plants.
So being aware of how you share your energy with others - is a very smart thing to know!

How you feel and act - will rub off on all other lives.
And how other people feel and act - can rub off on you.
So, if you are happy, healthy, loving, and good to yourself - everyone else around you – will feel the same way!

Remember how all the joyful critters in the woods - shared their energy with you - And how their joy, laughter, and dancing around - made you feel the same way?
You just couldn't help yourselves - you began laughing and dancing too!
Well, that is the energy cloud I speak of.

Now about the not-so-good energy.
When someone is being mean and hurtful - or causing harm to you - or another person - Or an animal - that is called a harmful energy cloud.

It makes no one feel good inside at all.
It is then you must be very strong and wise - And tell someone who has good wisdom and a good energy cloud about it.
Not speaking the truth - or keeping secrets - is not healthy or wise.
Especially if it hurts you - or someone else.

It is not ever okay to cause harm - or keep it a secret if you know about it.
Sharing the truth is the only way you can help yourself and others -
stay well, happy, wise, and loving.

Now, Children, do you understand this life mystery?"
At the same time, Whitney and Grayson both said, "Oh, yes, Magical Woman. We understand so much about life now"!

Grayson said, "So if we don't speak the truth when people cause harm - we won't be using good energy to help people, right"?
The Magical Woman said, "Oh Grayson, You are so very wise - And absolutely correct!"

Whitney said, "But, Magical Woman, I was always told not to tell secrets to anyone. But the wisdom you have shared with us - makes so much more sense"!

The Magical Woman goggled and said, "Think about it, wise children.
How will people become wiser and stronger - if no one shares their true thoughts?
How will people become safe and protected - if no one shares their true feelings?

Just like today, here with us - if we didn't share our secret mysteries with you - you wouldn't have learned so much - And, you wouldn't have known how special you are, right?!
If you don't share what you think and feel - then how will anyone grow to be strong, wise, and safe?"

Whitney said, "Wow! - I guess they wouldn't!
I understand now how important it is - to tell the truth!
I have seen people be mean and hurtful - And harm people and animals before.
And they asked me to keep it a secret too.

I didn't know we were supposed to share our true thoughts - so we could help others become strong, wise, and safe.
But I do now! - And I will definitely share from now on!"

Grayson said, "Oh, yes, Meeee too! Thank you, Magical Woman - we understand so much now."

The Magical Woman said, "Oh, Little Angels - you are most welcome.
Now, come walk with me through the woods."

The Magical Woman led Whitney and Grayson deeper into the woods.
Then when they reached a clearing in the center of the forest - they stopped walking.

Whitney and Grayson felt a very strange feeling move inside of them - And silence filled the air as they watched the Magical Woman with pure focus.

The Magical Woman closed her eyes and held her face up to the sky -
And a bright beam of sunlight - shined down upon her face from the sky.
She then took a slow deep breath - Innnn and ouuut.

As she stretched out her arms - her colorful wings lifted up into the air - And they began to flutter.
Then, she spoke to the sky - with a very strange bird-call sound.
She called out - "Ha-caw, Ha-caw, Ha-caw."

The Magical Woman of the Forest said, "Children, look to the sky and watch."
Whitney and Grayson were filled with curiosity - as they watched the sky.

At first, all they saw was a beautiful purple and blue sky.
But then - the sky mysteriously changed into all the colors of the rainbow.
It was the most beautiful sky they had ever seen.

Then, out of nowhere - they saw four magical Phoenix birds appear.
They were gliding through the air - dancing together.
They looked like huge, beautiful, magical dragons - flying through the rainbow sky.
And their tremendous wings - glistened and sparkled like diamonds in the sunlight.

Whitney and Grayson just stood there - watching their magical flight - in total awe of what they were seeing.
It felt like they were standing in a completely different world.
And they were.

Then, one by one - each phoenix bird landed - one in each corner of the woods.

Then, like a symphony of music - they all said together - at the very same time... "Magical greetings to you - our name is Miranda Ruby - And we have come to share a very powerful life mystery with you.

The phoenix ask you to remember - that life is made for you to feel like you are flying.
It is not made for upset - or for fighting yourselves or others.

Like us, your mind is made to fly with magic - And great wisdom.
Like all things - you are each made with special gifts - from the very day you were born.
One of those gifts - is to see the magic and beauty of nature - in every moment.
Another gift, and the most important of all - is to see, hear, and know only the good things.

It is that gift that blesses you with the greatest gift of all - which is Love.
It is then - you will fly high in all that you are - And all that you do."

The Miranda Ruby Phoenix began to flap their enormous wings - And all together - in one voice - they said, "Keep your hearts open so you may fly high dear ones - for there are no limitations to what you can be."

Then, they all lowered their heads - And closed their wings around their mystical bodies - And stood still in silence - like cocooned statues.

A BASKET FULL

OF MYSTERIES

Now Grayson, being the thinker, said, "Ohhhh, I soooo want to fly with peace- And great wisdom like the Phoenix!
I want to always see, hear, know and love - just like I did the day I was born."

The Magical Woman giggled and said - "All living things can - because being able to see, hear, and know love - never goes away.
After all, living things were not made to be any other way!
All anyone has to do is remind themselves that they know love."

Whitney said, "Oh, Magical Woman, I want everyone to feel all this magical greatness inside of them!
I don't want people or animals - to ever feel unhappy or unloved."

The Magical Woman then said - "Dear one, that wish is exactly what knowing love is about - And all the goodness love brings - is like a basket filled with treats!
And, you who doesn't love - love treats - for goodness sake!"

Then, Grayson asked - "Well, why don't people use their and greatness, good wishes, and love ALL the time - so they can enjoy a good and happy, loving life?"

The Magical Woman said, "Oh my, what an excellent question!
The reason is quite simple - it is because people forget to pay attention to themselves.

They forget their Spirit-heart - their inside self.

And when people forget about their inside self - they forget all about the most precious - good things in life."

Whitney said, "But, Magical Woman - why do we forget?"
The Magical Woman took a step backward - And raised her right arm to the sky as if she was calling something to her.

She then said - "Children, I will let two of my very special friends - share with you - Why people forget their inside self."
Just then, two very large, very wise, Turkeys flew in - And landed on the Magical Woman's right arm.

The turkeys puffed out their chests - stuck out their booty - And fanned their tail feathers out - far and wide.
Then, together, they said - "Gobble-gobble - little chillens - weeee, are the Todderics - And have Weeeee got the answer for you!

Gobble, Gobble, and Turkey Tails.
People forget their greatness - And inside selves because they are too focused on everything else - Or - what everyone else is doing.

And - when they peck and peck - worrying about unimportant things.
And - when they scratch and scratch - thinking about what other people will think and say.

And - sometimes when they are sick or don't feel good too.
But those are exactly the times people need the inside self - to help take away the blues!

So see, when you are busying your mind with outside stuff - that is not helping your health - that is just quite UN-natural, you see!
Because you were made - to enjoy your inside self - And take care of your mind and body in good ways!
If you don't do that - how do you expect to have happy, healthy days?"

Whitney said, "Oh, Todderic Turkeys - now, that must be another life mystery too - because that is very helpful and wise."

The Todderic Turkeys laughed with a gobble-gobble- gobble, and said,
"Why yes! Yes, Whitney - when you are right, you are right!"

Whitney then asked the turkeys - "But, I have a question. What does UN-natural mean?

The Todderic Turkeys both said together – at the same time - "Ahhh yes!
Let us share our turkey wisdom with you.

Knowing what is natural and UN natural - is very important - because it will help you make the wisest decisions as you grow up.

Now, when something is natural - it is exactly the way it was from the day that it was born - before people did something to change it.

Like a plant - it is natural because it grows in the ground - And nature feeds it with light, rain, and soil.
But it is unnatural when people add fertilizer to it or water it with processed water.

Natural is also like you were when you were born - And your inside self - And Angels too.
Your inside self and Angels are natural because people can't change them.

UN-natural is when people forget their inside selves - Or - when they pretend to be someone they are not - Or - when they say things that are untrue.
When something is UN-natural, you will always feel it inside.
Especially when it doesn't match who you are - And who you want to be."

Grayson said, "Yes! - I was just wondering about that today!
So people who act unhappy, unloving, and mean - have forgotten their natural way of being wise, happy, and loving.
They are being UN-natural - And will probably grow up to be unhappy, unloving people - right?!"

Just as Grayson finished saying that - A very wise, old Owl flew in - And perched upon a tree branch in front of them.

He hooted a - "Whoo - Whoo" - And said - "You are AbsoloHOOTly correct!

Greetings Children! - I am the wise Adamcarl Owl of the forest -
Whoooooo just so happens to have another life mystery to share with you!

When you love yourself - And all other life - then it is AbsoloHOOTly impossible - for you to grow up to be unhappy, unloving adults!

I will share another mystery with you too.
The magic people find in life is quite simple! - it's all about what is in your brain!

You will always be - exactly who you think you are!
You will always feel - exactly as you believe you feel!
You will always see and know what you want to be true.

So it would be very wise of you - to think - believe - and want only the good stuff about yourselves!"

Whitney asked the wise old owl - "But great Adamcarl owl - how can we be natural - and think good stuff - when so many people are teaching us the not-so-good stuff?"

The great Adamcarl Owl said, "Ah, magnificent question, magnificent question! You are very, very wise indeed, little lady!
All the good stuff is already inside of you!
It's how you are made, so it's really not very hard to do!

You can always be your natural self - just by knowing the not-so-good stuff - just isn't good for you!

Remember this too - when you know that what other people think, say, and do is their way - And Not your way - you will be your natural self.

Whitney said, "Oh, I understand - I understand! - Thank you! - And my, Oh my, what a very wise owl you are!

Right then -
  all the Aaliyah butterflies -
    and all the Miranda Ruby phoenix -
      and the Todderic turkeys -
        and the Adamcarl owl -
Yelled out at the very same time - "Hip-Hip-Hooray!"

Then, the Magical Woman said - "Lovely children - you have now reached an even greater life mystery - which is understanding.

Understanding all things have their ways - And all things are different for a very magical reason - gives you great power to make wise decisions.

Understanding things before accepting them - helps you choose what you want - And don't want to experience.

Most importantly - Understanding is a part of love - that keeps people together.
And, Oh - it's what keeps you in togetherness with the Angels too!"

JUST KNOWING THINGS

Grayson said, "Well, I understand that I want everyone to love and be in togetherness - with each other - And the Angels!"
He then said, "Magical Woman, I have a question.
Are the Angels - like Super-heroes?"

The Magical Woman giggled and said, "Oh, yes! Why they are the most superb super-heroes - of all the super-heroes - of all the universes - of all times!"

Whitney said, "But I thought Angels only lived in heaven!"

The Magical Woman gently raised her wings and said - "Children, look into my wings, and you will see."
Whitney and Grayson looked into her wings - And they saw a group of Angels - all lit-up - inside her wings!

The Magical Woman of the Forest said, "You see children,
Angels have extraordinary jobs keeping people, nature, and time in balance.
So they can be anywhere - And in any time.
They can be in anything - like an animal - a plant - a person - a shooting star - the wind - light - water or anything!

At that very moment - a herd of happy deer galloped through the forest.
They stopped and stood before Whitney and Grayson.

They all said together, at the very same time, "Greetings, children! -
Our name is Sophia - And we come to share another wisdom about the Super-Angels.

The super Angels are known as Archangels.
They are the most powerful Angels because - they know what is going to happen in all places - And in all times – even before it happens!

So they are always ready and prepared to help all living things.
You can feel their presence with you the most - when you are quiet, natural, and peaceful inside.

Each Angel helps nature, people, animals, and everything - everywhere - keep themselves natural and peaceful inside.
They often bring good blessings - And help every living thing move through life challenges.

They even help people have excellent ideas and talents - so you can help others.
Most importantly, the Angels help you understand that like them, you too - have a very special life and reason for being alive.

The Angels are always aware of you - and everyone - and everything - even when you are not."

Grayson then asked - "Sophia deer, then why don't they help adults take care of their problems?"

The Sophia deer chuckled and said, "Oh, dear Grayson, they do!
They especially help adults!

But, you see - people must be able to recognize when the Angels are near trying to help them - And many adults do not see this.

Adults often create their own problems because they forget to be aware - of the things, they can't see happening.
When they muddy up their minds - with troubled thoughts - And unkind thinking - they forget their happy, Angel-like, inside selves.

Adults sometimes let their brains get stuck in believing in their problems - instead of believing in what is good and truthful.
All of this - is why they can't see the Angels trying to help them."

Now, Whitney and Grayson knew the Sophia deer were speaking the truth - because they could feel it inside.
Plus, they are children - so it's easier for them - to see and believe in the magic of life.

They also knew it was true - because they have seen adults forget and ignore so many things - Especially when they are upset or worried.
A lot of the time they don't recognize anything or anyone else at all.
Not even themselves.

Just then, all the Allison raccoons run up and say - "Oh, yeah, and also, also, also - some adults don't even see that what they were worried about - always just magically goes away!
And if they do recognize it - they think that THEY were the ones who took care of it!"

All the critters in the woods began laughing out loud - And the entire forest echoed with the loudest laughter anyone had ever heard!

They were all laughing because most people don't know - that it may have been Angels who helped fix their problems!

The silly Allison raccoons were - rolling on the ground laughing out loud!
And the Todderic turkeys were gobble-laughing too!

Then, all of a sudden - the laughter abruptly stops.
Every critter - And every sound in the forest - went silent.
Whitney and Grayson noticed that all the animals - And all the trees in the woods - begin to sloooowly sway - back and forth.

And together - everyone started humming a beautiful, lovely sound.
It sounded like it was coming straight from heaven!
The heavenly sound echoed throughout the woods - And it was coming from above the trees.
The beautiful humming got louder – and louder – filling every space in the woods.

The Magical Woman then said - "Children, close your eyes - listen carefully - And you will feel her."

Whitney and Grayson closed their eyes and listened very carefully - And just when they were totally focused on the humming -
They heard only one heavenly, majestic voice singing a precious lullaby.

The sound of her lullaby spun and swirled - into a gentle blowing cone of wind.
And as her musical wind moved through the forest - her voice went into everything that heard it.

It went into Every tree -
   Every flower -
     Every animal -
       Every bird -
         Every insect -
           Every fairy -
And then, her precious lullaby went into Whitney and Grayson.
Her voice was like a soft blowing breeze - humming inside of them.
They felt like they were being filled up - with oodles of peace and love.

And the forest - And every critter
   And every tree - And the ground
     And the air - And the sky
       And the rocks - And waters
         All became filled with the peace and love of her voice.

Whitney said, so calmly, "Oh, My, Magical Woman of the Forest - who is that mystical voice that moves inside of us and everywhere?"

The Magical Woman said, "That my dearies, is Mother Universe.
She is made up of the nature of all things - from the beginning of time.

She knows and understands all things - All that ever was - is - and will be - because it is all stored within her lovely voice - As nature.

And every time she sings her precious lullaby through nature - her wisdom magically goes into all living things.
Her name is - Mother universe, Lauralisa."

Just then - Lauralisa, Mother Universe, began speaking her wisdom.
She said - "Blessings to you All - beautiful children of nature.
I am Lauralisa - and yet, I am also Mother Universe.

Just as I love and care for all living things - you, too, are made to do the same.
The circle of life is nature - And nature is made of love.
All things natural are very important - because it is the circle of love - that protects everything.

There are many natural things inside of you - that you will not be able to see with your eyes.
But, just know - you are nature - and you are love."

Love is in every living thing throughout nature - which means everything has its own heavenly melody to sing - And that includes you.
One day you will hear your precious melody singing inside of yourself - And you will know pure love - And know you must follow your heart. Please do so.

Whitney said, "Oh, Magnificent Mother Universe, how will we know the melody, and how do we follow our heart?"

Lauralisa, Mother Universe, whispered in the wind and said - "Why, darling, you are also part of the beginning of time.
So inside, you already know many things - you don't even think you know.

You will know the heavenly melody within you - when you are in nature - And feel nature's pure love fill you up.

Grayson then asks, "But, Mother Universe - how will we know that it's your voice inside of us?"

Mother Universe said - "Oh, children, you will always know my voice.

I will be the beautiful, calming, good thoughts - that come into your head.

My voice will be the happy feelings that fill you inside - And the love you feel when you look at a precious baby puppy or kitten".

I will be the loving voice that guides you to help nature and living things in need - And the peace you feel in your heart - when you lay your head to rest.

I will be your voice that is so thankful - for even the smallest things.

And - you will hear my voice whispering proudly through the wind - each and every time, you believe in yourself.

Then, as her voice began fading away, she said - I will remind you of the gift of silence - when you want to say something unkind.

And, in upsetting times - you will hear me say inside of you - have peace and love - And do what the Angels would do."

Then, her majestic voice became silent - And she became one the sky.

And just as she disappeared - a thousand tubes of light - began streaming into the woods.

A UNIVERSE

OF

MEMORY DUST

Each tube of light streaming into the woods - were beaming down like rods - And they were see-through. It was like looking into crystal balls.

When Whitney and Grayson looked through one tube - they could see the reflection of four Angels - And a magical world inside.
Then, something odd happened.

All the happy little Jessica fairies - began flying through the air.
And, one by one, they each flew into the see-through tubes of light.
They would stay inside the tube for a few seconds - And then fly back out again.

In and out they went.
And whenever they came back out - they were giggling - And sprinkling sparkly rainbow dust - all over the place.

The fairies flew past Whitney and Grayson and said, all together - "Now that's an experience - you must try!
Come on, kids – close your eyes - so you can see inside the tubes of light.

Whitney and Grayson closed their eyes - And they began to see a vision, like a dream - of a magical world.

This world had sparkling crystal skies - And rivers made of liquid gold - And joyful, tiny, singing hummingbirds - flying all around.

Whitney and Grayson saw a million fairies flying around too.
They were throwing some kind of shiny, sparkling dust on them.

Then, after a minute or so – Whitney and Grayson shook their heads - as if they were waking up and said, "Woah! Awesome! Magical Woman what is that sparkly dust the fairies were sprinkling on us?"

The Magical Woman giggled and said, "Why, that darlings, is called memory dust!
It helps you remember - love - your heart - And your special dreams.
Memory dust also helps you know that Angel magic is always within you.

But, the most magical thing about memory dust - is that it helps you see the Angels when they appear in your life.
And, it doesn't ever fade away either.
Memory dust, like the Angels - stays within you forever."

Now, Grayson had a confused look on his face - because he didn't quite remember seeing the Angels appear.
But - Miss Whitney did!

She said - "I do remember hearing an Angel say - "when we don't feel good, or we feel heavy - like there is no sunlight inside of us - we should close our eyes - And remember what the Woodland Angels have shared with us. Then, we will feel the light shine in us again.

Just then - two very wise squirrels hopped up on a tree branch - And they said, "Hello, there little ones - Our name is Shawnshawn,

And weeee know a mystery too - about how to make the light inside of you shine!
Do you want to hear it - Huh? Huh? Wanna hear it?"

Whitney and Grayson, of course, said - "Oh, yes, yes, we surely do!"

So, the Shawnshawn squirrels fluffed up their furry tails - stuck them straight up in the air - And sat upon a branch.
Then they folded their tiny little squirrel hands - over their little round bellies.

Then, they cleared their throats - looked at each other, and giggled.
They said, together - "Now about that mystery - What was it again?!

Oh, yes, yes, the mystery, Isssss - to eat nuts all day!"
The Shawnshawn squirrels busted out laughing - because they were just being silly.

Then they said - "No, Noo, Nooo - Now, seriously, seriously, seriously -
The reeeal mystery, Isssss - don't crack nuts with your teeth - they might break!"

Now, all the critters in the forest busted out laughing - And the Shawnshawn squirrels were laughing so hard - they almost fell off their tree branch!

Then, they said - "No, No, Nooo - We're just messing around!
Seriously, seriously, seriously - The REAL mystery of how to make the light shine issss...

When you are feeling dark and yucky inside – think and do only the things that make you feel good and sparkly inside!"

The Shawnshawn squirrels said - "Let us explain.
You can change any icky feelings and thoughts - in an instant - by doing something that you love or something you haven't done before.
Then, the yuckies magically go away - And you will feel all shiny!

You must know, too - that yucky life experiences also happen for a magical reason.
Understanding how something yucky can help you grow - is the greatest life wisdom you can have.
Life things happen for you - so you can learn and grow to be your most fabulous best self!

So - most yucky things aren't really all that bad - because they will help you become wiser and grow strong.
This is important too - because what you experience in life - also helps other people learn how to shine in themselves!"

The Shawnshawn squirrels then said, "That issss, of course - why you came into the woods today - isn't it?
You wanted to understand why people don't act happy and loving - like they did when they were children, right?!

Grayson said, "Oh, Yes sir, Shawnshawn squirrels - Yes sir!"
The Shawnshawn squirrels said, "Well, then - There ya go!
People don't act happy and loving - because they don't understand they can choose to be what they want.

They can shine with love and joy - if they understand how to grow wise and strong from yucky situations!
Understanding is one of the greatest super-powers!"

Whitney and Grayson understood what the Shawnshawn squirrels were telling them.
Grayson even thought to himself - he now understood why his family argues - And why some people are just not nice.

Grayson said, "Oh, Shawnshawn squirrels - I Get It! - Upset people just don't use their good selves and understanding - to fight the yuckies away!"

Just as Whitney and Grayson were thanking the Shawnshawn squirrels - for sharing their great wisdom - they heard something small - running through the woods.
They looked around to see who it was.
Why it was the Magical Woman's little Angel dog, Doodlekobi!

Doodlekobi runs up to Whitney and Grayson - And does a little dance for them.
He dances only on his hind legs - as his front legs swoop through the air.
His eyes are closed - and his nose is up to the sky!

Doodlekobi then sits down by their feet - And Whitney and Grayson knelt down to pet him.
Of course, he jumped up and gives them both - A big, wet, sloppy puppy dog kisses.

Doodlekobi then laid down on the ground, crossed his legs, and said -
"Whitney and Grayson - I have a very special mystery to share with you.

You see - life experiences are really - your invisible teacher.
You see, your brain has two sides - one side - lets you see and understand things with your eyeballs.
That side is the world that you play in each day.

And, the other side helps you see and understand things - you don't see.
That is the invisible world of knowing and feeling. We call that world your Spirit or inside self.

The invisible world is where the Spirits of the Angels - your family - friends - animals - And your pets live - who no longer live on Earth.

You may not be able to see them - But they can still see, hear and know you. What you can see with your eyes is what helps you live life - but it is what you can't see that keeps you - always - in togetherness."

Grayson said, "Oh, Doodlekobi, if we can't see the invisible world - how will we know the Spirit of the people we love - who have gone to heaven - are alive and okay?"

Doodlekobi said - "Oh well, That is easy! - You simply trust the signs you receive from them!
You must also trust that you are always together with them - because your Spirits are forever connected with love.

Trust helps you see and understand the hidden truth!

After all, it is all the things that we don't see with our eyes - that make life magical.

Now, Whitney began thinking quietly to herself.
She understood and trusted her inside feeling today - when she picked up the rock that had Angel wings on it.

She just knew deep inside of herself - that those wings were a sign.
She knew inside that rock was an invisible message - And a very special sign.

She thought - "That's exactly what understanding and trusting the invisible world means - And everything she thought - came true - because they have had a whole day of very special things happening.
And they were definitely feeling fantastic!"

Just then, Doodlekobi giggled with a Whuuuf, Whuuuf, and said - "Why, Yes, Whitney - that is exactly what it all means!"

Whitney giggled shyly and said, "But, Doodlekobi, I didn't say what I was thinking - out loud!
How did you know what I was saying inside myself?"

Grayson said, "I didn't hear her say anything either! How did you hear what she said inside of her head - Doodlekobi, can you read minds?"

Doodlekobi laughed with a Roooo, Roooo, and said – "Not exactly, my dearies. I don't read minds - but I can hear your Spirit and feel your energy.

It's all the stuff everyone shared with you today - all rolled into one thing called intuition.
Intuition is when you trust your knowing and understand your inside self.
It's a natural blessing that is inside of you - And every living thing!

And - that is how the Spirit of your loved ones - who have gone to heaven - stay with you too.

Grayson then said - "Woah! I soooo want to be able to trust and understand my intuition. My grandpa went to heaven - And I miss him so much.
Can I still talk to him and feel him?

Doodlekobi said, "Why, of course, you can!
The Angels - And your loved ones in heaven can hear and feel you just like I did - And, you can hear and feel them too.

Remember, just because your eyeballs can't see them - it doesn't mean they don't exist or are gone - they simply just go invisible.
All you ever need to do - is feel togetherness with your Grandpa - And you will feel him with you.

No matter what - you are not ever separate from heaven - Or the people who have gone to be their Spirit self.

There are many invisible mysteries in life - And a lot of things you won't ever see or know - because there's no way that your eyes can see everything - in all the worlds.
But - you can know and trust one thing for sure - you are not ever alone.

You always have togetherness with the invisible world - even if you can't see it, hear it, or touch it!"
That is what makes life so magical!

You can't see the air, wind, space, invisible bugs - Or - even the organs inside of your body - but they are all there - real and alive!

Whitney then said, "But, Doodlekobi - if someone goes to the invisible world of heaven - how can we still be together - if we can't touch them - or hug them?"

Doodlekobi said - "Oh, now, that's easy-peasey!
Everything and everyone - are together at all times - And forever - by Love!
Love an invisible string - holding everything in togetherness - And it is the most powerful energy of all!

Now, you can't really see or touch love - but you can feel it and hold it in your heart and mind.
So all you have to do is feel love in your heart and mind for those in heaven - And as you love them - they will feel it too!

Have no worries, dear children - everyone in heaven - even your pets - are still together with you - by the invisible string of love."

Grayson then said, "Wow! I never knew about these things - life really is amazing!
I have a friend at school whose dad went to heaven to be his Spirit self.
And he told me that he could feel his dad near him all the time.
I didn't understand how that could be - but now I do!

Thank you so very much, Doodlekobi, for helping us understand.
Knowing this warms my heart - And now I understand what my friend means when he feels his dad.

Doodlekobi let out a howl and said, "Ooooowwwwww, you are most welcome!
And remember - life is veeeeery mysterious - we ALL live the mystery of life Together - even if we can't see it."

Just then, Doodlekobi, and Whitney, and Grayson - And all the critters in the forest felt a soothing, loving warmth - come down from the sky - and fill up the woods.

Everyone closed their eyes - And lifted their faces to the sky - in silence.
They all stood there - feeling the invisible string of love and togetherness - fill the air - And move through them.

It was the most magical feeling they had ever felt.

Maybe you should close your eyes for a moment and feel it too!

THE KEEPERS

OF THE SPIRIT

After a few moments feeling the invisible string of love and togetherness - everyone opened their eyes and just smiled.

They all looked over at the Magical Woman of the Forest. She was standing in the center of the woods now.

Her eyes were closed - And she held her face up to the sky.
Her arms were stretched out wide as if she was hugging the world.
Then, she began twirling around in a circle.

As she twirled - round and round - electrified streaks and glowing, green, fairy dust - began streaming out of her hands.

The strings of electricity - were like lightning - dancing through the air.
And the forest was filled with so much glowing fairy dust - that Whitney and Grayson couldn't see anything else.

All of a sudden - The strings of lightning danced into everything.- And the fairy dust made every space glow like glow-worms.
Whitney and Grayson even glowed too!

Then, a beautiful Spirit appeared through the cloud of fairy dust.
And she said - "Hello, children - I am Geri, the Spirit of the Earth.
I have come to share a very important mystery with you - about belief.

When you believe what you feel inside - even if it doesn't make sense right away - you will always know the truth that's inside you.
Whenever you don't understand something - and you are confused - you must believe that the Angels are near helping to bring understanding to you.
When you believe in what <u>you</u> know - great peace will always be in your heart."

Then - Spirit of Earth, Geri - gently floated up into the air.
And as she began fading into the beautiful sky - she said - "Remember to always believe in yourselves."
And Poof - she turned into a cloud of glowing fairy dust - and disappeared.

Then, A quiet falling rain came into the forest. Everyone was being misted with water from the rain.

And another Spirit appeared through the cloud of fairy dust - And she said - "Hello, I am Boni, Spirit of the Water. I have come to share a very important mystery with you about harm.

"You already know inside what makes you a good and decent person - And being a good person - doesn't mean being dishonest or causing harm to yourself, other people - or any living thing.
That is not the way you are made to be.
You are made to be kind and loving to all things - including yourselves."

Then - the Spirit of water, Boni - turned into one tiny little raindrop - And she said - "always choose to be better."

Then, she evaporated into the air - And disappeared.

Then, A soft blowing wind blew over Whitney and Grayson - And another Spirit appeared through the cloud of fairy dust.

And she said, "Hello children, I am Jennifer, the Spirit of the Air.
And I come to share with you the mystery of Love.

When you understand that all of your experiences are to help you grow - you will truly know the power of Love.

Because loving your life experiences - even the not so enjoyable ones - help you love life and yourself.
And, when you can love life and yourself - you can love everything and everyone.

All you, people, and animals, and even plants need - is to feel loved.
So if you - or anyone ever feels icky - break out the love, and everyone will feel better again."

Grayson said, "Yes, yes, Spirit Jennifer of the Air - I understand!
I have seen people get upset and act mean and unloving to each other.
Then, after they apologize and make up with each other, they do feel better!"

Whitney then said, "Ummm, Spirit Jennifer, I have a question.
Why don't the Angels just make people feel love all the time?
Then, everyone can always be happy and loving."

Spirit Jennifer said, "Oh, lovelies, I must go and allow the next Spirit to answer your question."

Spirit Jennifer of the Air - swirled herself into a blowing wind - And as she began to fade away, she said - "Remember, everything was created with Love, As love. "

And her wind blew away - And she disappeared.

Just then, A ray of sunlight beamed into the forest - And in the sunbeam, a Spirit appeared.

And she said - "Hello, I am Faith, the Spirit of the Fire.
I come to share the mystery to your question, Whitney.

Angels will not make people do things because - people must first want it from their heart.

Angels will only remind you - to choose good things for yourselves.
If you want to love - And be loved - Or - you want to help people by doing good work like the Angels do - then the Angels can help you with that.

If you want a toy, wish, or something for yourself - the Angels can help you with that too - But, those kinds of wants - are called blessings.

Angels offer blessings when people have filled themselves - And other lives with Love, like the Angels, do.

Then the Spirit Faith, of Fire - floated gently back into the sun's ray - And as she faded away, she said - "Always want blessings and goodness to be your way of life."

And her sunbeam blended with the sun - And she disappeared.

Now, all the critters in the forest - began clapping and jumping up and down with excitement and joy.
They were all - so very proud of the magnificent job they did - sharing their wise mysteries with Whitney and Grayson.
All the critters started patting each other on the back - And giving each other - hi-fives and hugs - for a job well done.

Then, the Magical Woman of the Forest led Whitney and Grayson over -
to a very large rock - that sat in the North end of the woods. The magical Woman asked them to sit upon the rock - And get comfortable.

They did - And as they looked around - they noticed that there was a beautiful mystical garden across from them.
It had the most beautiful blue sparkling waterfall they had ever seen.

And next to the waterfall - there was also a very large dark cave.
The cave was covered - with all different kinds of brightly colored plants and vines.

And all the plants - were gently swaying back and forth - as if they were dancing to the sound of the splashing waterfall.
It really did look like a place straight out of heaven!

Just then - all the woodland critters became veeeery quiet.
And an eerie silence moved through the forest again.

Then, another rough - and tumble - loud rumble - came out of the old, ancient tree.

Whitney and Grayson looked over at the tree - And they saw the tree had turned into a bright, solid white light.
It was so bright and white - that they had to put their hands over their eyes for a moment.

Then - BAM! - five floaty things that looked like huge bubbles - popped out of the old tree.
The floaty bubble things began to circle around Whitney and Grayson.

Then, they sped up - And made even faster circles around them - as fast as fast can be - Zoom - Zoom - Zoom!
They were spinning circles around Whitney and Grayson so fast - Whitney and Grayson got dizzy!
And the floaty bubble things - were shooting out glittery dust everywhere.

This dust wasn't like the fairy dust, though.
It felt different - because it was kind of sticky - And it was shaped like glittering gold and silver stars.

But, the most amazing thing about this dust was - it was singing!
Just like a choir of Angels!

Whitney and Grayson were amazed - And just stood there and watched -
as the glittering dust had fun - dancing and singing in the air.

Whitney said, "Magical Woman, what kind of fairy dust is this? It's so amazing!"

The Magical Woman said - "Oh, sweety, that isn't fairy dust – Oh, no, no, no!
That - is a very special dust from the beginning of time.
THAT - is Archangel dust, my darlings!

This Angel dust is made from the light of ALL the Angels - everywhere - And it's filled with all of their love, wisdom, and special powers!"

Just then, Whitney and Grayson saw one floaty bubble thing float by - And it went right into the sparkling blue waterfall - And disappeared.

Then, another floaty thing floated by them - And went into the large cave.
And, another floaty thing floated by - And went back into the old ancient tree.
And then another floaty thing drifted right into the large rock - that Whitney and Grayson were sitting on!

Whitney and Grayson, at the very same time, said - "WHOA! Magical Woman, what are those floaty bubble things?

Just then, all the forest critters started to get antsy.
They were becoming so very excited because - they knew what was coming next!

THE

MIGHTY WIZARD

MITCH

The Magical Woman giggled and said - "Those, sweet children - are the Archangels - Or what some people like to call The Super Angels!"

Grayson said, "But, Magical Woman, there were five Archangel floaty things that came out of the ancient tree. But, I only saw four go into things.
One went into the cave - another into the tree - another in the waterfall - And the fourth one went into the rock.
So where - And who - is the other Archangel?"

The Magical Woman giggled and said - "Ah, I see - you are very aware!
That floaty thing would be - The Great Magical Wizard Mitch!
He is the Angel Wizard who helps me prepare people - so they can understand the Archangels and their wise messages.

It usually takes him a few minutes to appear.
He flies around invisible at first - making sure that everyone is feeling love, happiness, and a magical heart.
Otherwise, he won't appear until everyone feels that way."

Just then - things got even more exciting!
Whitney and Grayson began to see his magic appear!

First - A magic wand appeared - floating right in front of them in mid-air!
  Then, A magician's hat appeared - And it was dancing up and down.
    Then, A magic cape appeared - And it was flapping like it was in the wind.

The Wizard's magic wand had glowing stars in it - And his hat had floating planets and comets on it - And his magical cape had glowing moons, suns, and shooting stars.
It was like looking right into outer space!

Then, Whitney and Grayson see the Wizard's arms appear - right in front of them.
One arm was just hovering right in mid-air!
Then, his legs appeared - And then half of his body.

And then, for goodness sake - only his eyeballs appeared!
They just floated right there - in mid-air - just looking around!

Now, Whitney and Grayson couldn't see his mouth - but they could hear him laughing hysterically at the surprised look on Whitney and Grayson's face!

The Magical Wizard, Mitch, finally - put all of his body parts together - And appeared as a whole person.
Then, the magician's hat jumped up into the air - And it flew over and landed on top of the Wizard's head.
Then, the cape flew over - And wrapped around his shoulders.
And the magic wand flew over - And hopped into his hand.

The Wizard Mitch smiled a great big shining smile – like he always does - And said - "Hi, kids! - I am the magical Wizard Mitch.
I help the people of the out-world prepare their minds and hearts - to meet the magnificent Archangels."

Whitney and Grayson said, together, with pure excitement - "Wow! - You are awesome! - we are so glad to meet you!
Magical Wizard, are you going to help us learn magical mysteries - so we can meet the Woodland Angels?"

The Wizard Mitch said - "Why, of course – of course!
I wouldn't be a very cool wizard - if I didn't have magical mysteries to share?!"

Then - the great and mighty Wizard Mitch - pulled off his Wizard's hat - And held it out in front of Whitney and Grayson.
He then said - "Children, look - look deep into the magic hat."

Whitney and Grayson, of course, looked really deeeep - into the hat!
And what do you think they saw?

They saw a reflection of themselves. It was like looking into a mirror.
They actually saw themselves - looking deeeeep into the magic hat!

Then, they saw a reflection of the rock they were sitting on - but the rock was now dark – And it had a million white flickering stars inside of it.
It looked just like the night sky.

Now, they could see themselves sitting on the rock - but their bodies were not shaped like their regular bodies.
Whitney and Grayson's bodies were now shaped like shining tubes of light!

Of course, they had to see what was what.

So they stopped looking into the hat and looked down at the rock - to see if what they saw in the hat - was really happening - And it was!

The rock they were sitting on - looked just like a star-filled night sky - And their bodies were glowing like tubes of light!

Whitney and Grayson giggled with amazement!
As they jumped off the rock, they said, together - "Wow!" Wizard Mitch! Your hat is so cool! - It's like a crystal ball!"

The Great Wizard giggled and said - "Oh, yes, it is - it is indeed!
A true Wizard's hat is absolutely a Wizard's crystal ball - And it's exactly how Wizards know so much.
My wise and wonderful wizard hat - shows me everything that the Angels see and know.

And that is why you can see your bodies as beams of light - because that is how the Angels see you.
And that is why I can be invisible - And do so many magical things - because I trust the invisible world!"

Right then, Whitney and Grayson yell out, at the same time - "I want one! Where can we get a magic hat like that?!"

The Wizard Mitch bent over laughing, holding his belly - And said - "Dear, Little Wizards - this magic hat was given to me by a superb Archangel Michael.
It magically appeared one day - so that I could use it - to help people believe in life's mysteries - And Angel wisdom.

Now, life can be as magical - as you want it to be.
It can be just so amazing - if you believe it is in your heart.

Like all the things you have experienced here today - every bit of mystery and magical wisdom is already inside of you.

Angels wisdom - helps you stay magical, wise, happy, and loving - just like the day you were born.
After all - it's the Angels who help you remember - your very own special power - so you may be a gift within the world.

Whitney then said, "But, Wizard Mitch - how will we know when the Angels are there helping us - And reminding us?"

The Great Wizard Mitch tossed his magic hat into the air - And it landed right on Whitney's head!
He said - "That, dear children, is the greatest mystery of all - for you to figure out!

Angels communicate by giving you signs and inside knowing.
You will know when Angels are helping you - when you are paying attention to their signs!

The rest is like a puzzle - you see.
You will spend your lifetime - putting the signs and your knowing together.

Then - Voila! You will just mysteriously know - exactly when the Angels are near helping you.

Angel signs appear in all kinds of ways - like the Angel's wings on the rock that Whitney found today.
And how my magician's hat - just appeared out of the blue.

Angels send messages to you through your dreams - And even conversations - when you are talking with other people.
Or - you just might have a very strong gut feeling - for no reason at all.

The most magical sign that an Angel is near - is when animals appear.
They love connecting with animals - because animals speak with energy and intuition instead of human words.

Angel's can give you messages through - movies, books, and songs too.
They can really - use just about anything - to get their love and wisdom to you!
But, the most important sign of all – is your inside knowing is always the best!"

Much like how the birds and animals in the wild just know when they must go home - or find shelter when a strong storm is coming. They just know.
Angels give you - the same inside knowing too."

Just then, the Wizard's magic wand - jumped up into the air - And swirled around.
Then it spoke! It said - "Oh, my, oh my - this is quite the puzzle, too - because the Angels can look like anything - even me and you!

They may be a person standing right in front of you one day - Or - an animal in the woods.

They might be a flower - a light - a floaty bubble thing - Or fairy dust!

They might be in the trees - Or looking through a waterfall - Or inside rocks and caves - Or - they could be in the sky, wind, ocean waves!
Well, for goodness' sake, Angels could even be a Santa Claus - ringing a bell here and there!
Angels are the invisible world soooo – they can be everywhere!"

Whitney and Grayson said, together - "Oh, Wow, we so want one of those - talking magic wands too!"

The Wizard Mitch laughed and said - "I bet - if you filled your hearts and minds with love - And paid attention to the Angel's signs - you both - may very well get a magic wand one day too!"

Then, a brilliant, shining green dust - began to swirl around in the woods -
And the Magical Woman said - "Weeeell children - your hearts and minds have been prepared - so that you can understand the Super Archangel messages. Are you ready to meet them now? - Or would you rather wait?"

Whitney and Grayson looked at each other with wide-eyed excitement - And said – "Pfft, Wait? No way! - Oh, yes, yes - we are sooooo very ready to meet them!"

The great Wizard Mitch said - "Well, all-righty then!
Whitney and Grayson, you must close your eyes - And place your hands upon the large sky rock."
So they did.

And just as they put their hands on the sky rock - the Wizard Mitch waved his magic wand in the air - over the rock.

And with a twist - And a twirl - full of magic and might - the woods came alive with most brilliant light!

And everyone in the forest sat silently - waiting to see - who the Magical Wizard Mitch would call into sight!

The great and powerful Wizard swirled his magic wand - round and round - through the air - And then, he said...

"Hocus Pocus - by the Wizardly blue skies
Let us all now see - beyond the eyes
Let us see - where great heavenly wings fly.
Oh, loving and true - mighty Angels - of all that is good and high
Won't you appear - before our loving smiles?"

Then, the magical Wizard - tapped his hat three times with his magic wand - And closed his eyes.
And every living thing in the woods - began to hum a soft melody into the air.

As their song echoed through the forest - like a beautiful breeze -
everyone could feel the love and magical power spread through the woods - And them.

THE

SUPER

ARCHANGELS

The ground began to rumble - And gently vibrate - And the trees swayed beautifully from side to side.

At that very moment, together, The Magical Woman - And the great Wizard Mitch spoke to the sky rock and said...

"Oh, Archangel Raphael, great healing wings of the sky - we ask of you, most good and high - won't you please come forth before our eyes?"

Just then, the star-filled sky rock burst open!
And all the stars that were inside the rock - exploded out into the woods floating in mid-air.

There were billions of sparkling stars - everywhere.
And then - out of the large sky rock - Archangel Raphael appeared.

This Angel had wings that were made of the whitest stars - you ever did see.
As Angel Raphael floated up in the air - like a scarf blowing in a gentle wind.

The Angel said... "My dear Whitney and Grayson - I help heal all life of their illnesses, wounds, and upsets.
I help you to know healthy wisdom - And how to heal your pains and upsets naturally.

To do this - just fill your minds with Angel thoughts - think like an Angel would do - And do natural things to keep your body and mind - strong and well.

Thinking good, loving, healthy thoughts - And knowing how greatly you are blessed at all times - is a great way to heal the body and mind.

Then, Archangel Raphael's star-filled wings opened up, wide - And a glittering blue Angel dust - floated gently out into the woods.

Whitney and Grayson felt so perfect inside.
They closed their eyes, held out their arms - And began twirling in the glittering Angel dust.

After a moment - Whitney and Grayson stopped - And together, they said - "Oh, Thank you, Thank you, Angel Raphael - for teaching us how to feel better!
We will always remember to have happy Angel thoughts and love ourselves - to keep ourselves healthy and well."

Then, Archangel Raphael slowly floated into the air above them.
Whitney and Grayson could feel the love and healing energy -
fill the woods - And move inside of them.

It felt like the greatest hug they had ever had!
And then Poof! - Archangel Raphael all the stars - And blue Angel dust disappeared.

Then, The Great Wizard Mitch said...
"Whitney and Grayson - Now, let us go meet the next Archangel at the mystical waterfall."

Now, everyone was standing quietly - in front of the beautiful glistening waterfall.
It was gushing, sparkling, blue-green waters - And it was so majestic and peaceful.

Together, the Magical Woman and the Wizard Mitch - spoke to the glistening waterfall and said - "Oh, Archangel Gabriel, great healing wings of the sky - we ask of you, most good and high - won't you please come forth before our eyes?"

Just then - the waterfall began to gush harder - And faster - And it became very loud.
Water was splashing everywhere!

The waterfall then exploded with the sound of a huge crashing wave - And out of the glistening waterfall, Archangel Gabriel appeared.

Whitney and Grayson stood there amazed - because this Angel's wings were singing!

Archangel Gabriel's wings had like a million voices - And they were whispering beautiful melodies - And filling the air with kind and gentle words.

Angel Gabriel floated up into the air - like a leaf dancing with the wind - And said - "My dear Whitney and Grayson - I am the Angel who helps you understand how to communicate with people, animals, and Angel guides.

I help you know how to speak the truth - And bring you knowledge so you may think bigger and better things for yourself.

When you communicate with yourself truthfully - And with kindness - you will be able to understand - exactly what people, animals, and Angel guides are sharing with you.

Kindness, truth, and understanding - gives you the most amazing relationships - And then - All harmful words disappear from your memory.

Then, Archangel Gabriel's wings opened up wide - And tiny pieces of silver and gold Angel dust sprinkled out into the woods.

This Angel dust was incredible - because it was shaped like tiny musical notes. And each speck of dust - played its own tone - And with all the Angel dust playing their sounds together - it made a symphony - of the most beautiful heavenly melody.

Whitney and Grayson feel so perfect inside.
They closed their eyes - held out their arms - And began twirling in the musical Angel dust.

After a moment, Whitney and Grayson stop twirling - And together, they said - "Oh, Thank you, Angel Gabriel, for sharing your heavenly wisdom!

We will always remember - to speak to ourselves just like we would if we were in heaven…. with kindness, truth, and understanding.
We love you, the Angels, ourselves, animals - And, well, everyone.
And we want to have wonderful relationships too!

Then, Archangel Gabriel slowly floated into the air above them.
And when Gabriel's magnificent singing wings spread out - far and wide - Whitney and Grayson could feel a million loving Angel words - speaking inside of them.
It felt like the kindest hug they had ever had!

And then Poof! - Archangel Gabriel, the heavenly melody - And all the loving Angel words - disappeared into the air.

Then, the Magical Woman of the Forest said - "Whitney and Grayson, you have received Archangel's Gabriel's heavenly secret - Now, let us go meet the next Archangel at the mysterious cave."

Everyone stood intrigued - in front of the mysterious cave - admiring its beauty and secrecy.

The cave was very dark and silent inside - but the plants that were around the cave - were shining bright - And full of life.
The plants were gently swaying back and forth - And they are all glowing with the most beautiful purple light.

Together - the Magical Woman and the Wizard Mitch spoke into the cave - and said - "Oh, Archangel Uriel, great cleansing wings of the sky - we ask of you, most good and high - won't you please come forth before our eyes?"

As Whitney and Grayson looked inside the dark cave - they saw a tiny, teensy, weensy, white light flash - deeeeep inside the cave.
And it became bigger - And brighter - as it moved towards them.

Then, a brilliant flash of light burst out of the cave - And the white light turned into a violet cloud of Angel dust.

And out of the violet cloud - Archangel Uriel appeared.
Now, this Angel had beautiful wings filled with glowing moons, planets, and shooting comets!

Angel Uriel floated up into the air - like a feather floating down a stream. The Angel then said - "My dear Whitney and Grayson - I protect the heavens - And help you cleanse your not so loving thoughts and actions.

I help you remember any not-so-good things you have done, said, or thought - so your heart may be clean and free to know the heavens.

When you have thoughts and do things that an Angel would not do - I help bring the light of awareness - to help cleanse those things from your body.

And I teach you to know the difference between - heavenly love - love that is good and safe for you - And the types that are not."

Then, Archangel Uriel's wings opened up - And sparkling violet Angel dust swirled all around Whitney and Grayson.
They closed their eyes - held out their arms - and began twirling in the glistening violet cloud that blanketed the forest.

Whitney and Grayson felt such deep heavenly love and protection - moving deep inside of them.
It felt like the safest hug they had ever had!
And then Poof! - Archangel Uriel and the sparkling violet cloud of Angel dust disappeared.

Now, Whitney and Grayson were still twirling - feeling Archangel Uriel's safe hug - after the Angel had disappeared.

When they stopped twirling - And saw the Angel was gone - they didn't feel good about it inside at all.
Whitney was quite upset and said, "Oh, No, Magical Woman - we didn't get to thank Archangel Uriel for teaching us to keep our hearts and minds clean.
Oh, No. We must give thanks - oh, please call Archangel Uriel back."

The Magical Woman of the forest said - "Now, now, children - do not worry yourselves a bit.
This moment is just another opportunity - to learn another life mystery.
You see, this life mystery is about the goodness of the heart.

In those times when you can't see with your eyes - you will always be able to feel with your heart.

Just like now - when you are unable to thank someone face-to-face. Just think about your gratefulness in your head - And feel your goodness and love in your heart - And then the Angels will make sure - the person receives your love.

You can do the same thing with the Spirit of people and animals you love after they have gone to heaven.

Whitney and Grayson then grab hold of each other's hands.
They close their eyes - And thought about how thankful they were for Angel Uriel's wisdom - And they began to feel the love and gratefulness warm their hearts.

Then, together - they said out loud - "Oh, Angel Uriel - Thank you for sharing your love, good wisdom, and heavenly protection.
We will always remember to think, act, and do our best - to feel the light and love of the heavens."

The Magical Woman of the Forest said, "Well now, children, that was beautifully said!"

Just then, a tremendous violet light lit up the woods.
The Magical Woman said - "See there, children - that violet light is a sign from Archangel Uriel - letting you know that your love and thankfulness was received!

Now that you have learned Angel Raphael's life mystery for healing -
And Angel Gabriel's life mystery for communication -
And Archangel Uriel's life mystery of heavenly love and protection -
Let us now meet the last of the "Woodland Angels."

Everyone then walked over to the magnificent, glowing ancient tree - And stood quietly before it.
Whitney and Grayson were mesmerized by the magnificent, brilliant, gold and white rays of light - beaming from the tree.

The old, ancient tree then began moving - as if it was breathing again.
But, this time, Whitney and Grayson could actually hear breath coming out of the tree - And they gasped in utter amazement.

The Magical Woman said - "Children, this glorious tree holds all the wisdom - of all the Angels - everywhere."

Then, she and the magical Wizard - placed their hands upon the tree.
They closed their eyes - And together they said - "Oh, glorious Archangel Michael great cleansing wings of the sky - we ask of you, most good and high - won't you please come forth before our eyes?"

Then, after a few moments - the tree began to shake - And all the leaves and branches lit up with the most beautiful, sparkling color of red they had ever seen.
Then, a beautiful red fog began to seep out of the tree bark - And out of the sparkling red fog - Archangel Michael appeared.

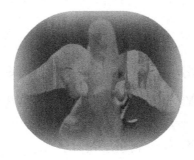

Now - this Angel was not like the others.
This Angel was the red fog - And the red fog was actually the Angels humongous wings.

The Angel's red fog wings - were actually feathers - And they looked like a horse's tail blowing in the wind.

Whitney and Grayson saw something else inside the red fog wings - so they looked closer. They saw that the wings had a million eyes inside.

Then, when Archangel Michael's wings moved, they made a tremendous sound. It sounded like a hundred horses galloping through the sky.

Whitney and Grayson were so amazed they just stood with their mouths open.

Then the red fog of Archangel Michael spoke and said - "I am Archangel who helps you understand how to guard and protect goodness and truth.
I help you understand how to help - All living things with love - And also fight to end harmfulness.

I teach you to know that you, too - are Angels of heavenly love and protection - And that you - And every living thing - has a very important purpose for being alive.
Remember this - And you will not ever feel defeated or unimportant.

Then, Archangel Michael's red cloud of Angel dust - swirled into a tornado.
   Then a tornado of blue Angel dust appeared -
      And then, a tornado of silver and gold Angel dust appeared -
         Then another tornado appeared, and it was made of violet Angel dust

This was such an amazing sight. But it really blew Whitney and Grayson's, minds - when the four tornados of Angel dust - shaped themselves into four enormous glittering horses!

Then, Whitney and Grayson watched the four Angelic horses - gallop off into the sky - and disappear.

They felt so magical inside - they closed their eyes and imagined - that they were riding on the glittering Angel horses.

They felt so brave and strong inside - it felt like an army of Angels were hugging them.

After a few moments, Whitney and Grayson sent their invisible thank you to the Angels.
They said, together, "Oh, Thank you, great Archangel guides - we will always remember - that we are made like the Angels ourselves.

Right then, the woods lit up - like one super-gigantic sparkler - And the sound of a hundred galloping horses echoed through the woods - And in the sky.

Whitney and Grayson knew that was a sign that the Archangels heard their thank you and felt their love.

Then, a peaceful silence filled the woods - And Whitney and Grayson stood there feeling the perfect silence for a moment.

Then, they gave their most heartfelt thanks to the Magical Woman - And the Wizard Mitch - And all of the woodland critters - And everyone else they couldn't see with their eyes!

WE BID THEE FAREWELL

The Magical Woman and Wizard Mitch said, "Now, Whitney and Grayson, you are very wise and loving.
Now, dear children, it is time for us to say farewell.
We hope you will take all that you have learned here today into your heart - And share your love with others - so they might understand they are little Angels on Earth too."

Whitney and Grayson both said at the same time - "Awwwwe, But - we don't ever want to say goodbye to all of you!"

The Wizard Mitch said, "Oh, - No, No, No, Dear children - we don't ever say goodbye!
We always bid thee farewell – which means we will see each other again!"

Just then, a gusty wind blew through - And all the trees in the forest began to shake again.
And all the leaves and branches of every tree - lit up with the most beautiful rainbow of light.
Then, a fluffy white cloud - came down from the sky - And it spread out far and wide - And hovered in mid-air.

Then, All of Whitney and Grayson's new friends began to re-appear
  All the lights and floaty bubble things appeared.
    And all the moving shadows, mists, and swirls appeared.
      And all the Makaiya ladybugs.
        And all the Jacob glow-worms.
          And all the Jessica fairies appeared.

And all the Aaliyah butterflies appeared.
And all the yellow Payton flowers,
And all the Ryan earthworms,
And all the Brooklyn bunnies appeared.

And all the Emily foxes appeared.
And all the Allison raccoon,
And all the Rylee doves,
And all the Jonah honey bees appeared.
PHEW!
And the Miranda Ruby Phoenix birds appeared.
And the Sophia deer,
And the Adamcarl owl,
And the Todderic turkeys,
And the Shawnshawn squirrels appeared.

And Lauralisa, Mother Universe appeared.
And Geri, the Spirit of Earth,
And Boni, the Water Spirit,
And Jennifer, the Spirit of Air,
And Faith, the Spirit of Fire,
And then, Archangel Gabriel, Raphael, Uriel, and Michael appeared.

LAWDY, THAT'S A LOT OF NEW FRIENDS!

Then, everyone together, as one voice said - "We bid you farewell sweet children.
Remember you are wonderfully made - And know in every moment - that you are happy, loving, and worry-free.
Because that is exactly the way you were made to be!

Stay well with good thoughts - And always be true - because you just never know - when an Angel might be standing right in front of you!"

Then, all their new friends - blew Whitney and Grayson a forest full of Angel kisses - And Whitney and Grayson felt every one of those kisses inside!

The Magical Woman then closed her eyes- And she stretched out her arms. She began to spin - around and around - And glittering green fairy dust - streamed out of her hands into the air.

As she lifted her wings made of many colors - an emerald green smoke billowed out into the woods.
And Poof! - Everyone in the forest became invisible - And disappeared.

Now, Whitney and Grayson were left just standing there - alone, in the dark, quiet woods.
Grayson said - "Ummmm Whitney, how are we going to get back home?
We are so far into the woods – I don't know the way back to the out-world.

Whitney said, "Well, all of our new friends and the Angels - did say for us to use what we have learned today - And that the wisdom we need is already in us.

So - let's use our wisdom - think about good things - And believe that the Angels will show us the way home."

So they did.

They closed their eyes and thought about the Angels watching over them - And how they needed the Angel's guidance.

Then, after a few moments, a mysterious miracle happened - The Magical Wizard Mitch re-appeared!

He was smiling and said - "Good job Whitney and Grayson!
We are all so proud of you for using your inside wisdom!
And I am here to give you a ride back to the out-world!"

Whitney said, "Oh, Thank you, Wizard Mitch, for coming to help us!
And Grayson said, "Ummm, did you say ride? Are we going to take a magic carpet ride?!"

The fantastic Wizard Mitch said - "Why, of course!
Now, what kind of Wizard would I be - if I didn't give magic carpet rides!?"

Whitney and Grayson's eyes were as wide as could be - And they were, of course, about ready to burst open with excitement!

The Great Wizard Mitch then raised his magic wand - And he gave it a wiggle and a swirl - And a shake and a shimmy.

Then he said - "Razzle Dazzle - Bippity Boo - with fairy dust and Angel wings too!

Oh, magic carpet friend - good and high - won't you come true - so that we may fly with you in the sky!"

Then, a fluffy white fog appeared in the air - And POOF!
There was a magic carpet - hovering right above their heads.

Whitney and Grayson thought this magic carpet was so cool - because it was made of Angel dust - And it was surrounded by a fluffy white sparkling cloud.

But, the coolest thing of all was that it had Angel wings on the sides of it!
One wing had bright stars - And another wing was singing -
And another wing had glowing moons, planets, and shooting comets - And the other wing was a like a horse's tail - with a million eyes in it!

The Magical Wizard Mitch then took his magic wand - And tapped Whitney and Grayson on the head - And they magically began to float slowly up into the air.
They started giggling - because it felt funny - to be all wobbly.
Then, the Wizard Mitch sat them gently upon the magic carpet.

And boy, Ohhhhh boy, did Grayson love this magic carpet - because he felt like he was sitting high up in a treetop.
And Whitney loved it too - because she could feeeel - all the magical energy inside the carpet.

Then, Whitney and Grayson looked down into the magic carpet - And what they saw - was most definitely a mystery!
They saw that they weren't actually sitting on a carpet at all!
There was nothing there!
There was no bottom!

It was completely invisible!
They were just floating in mid-air!
Just then, all of their new forest friends began to appear inside the invisible, bottomless carpet!
They were all waving farewell and blowing sweet kisses to Whitney and Grayson.

Then, in a puff of smoke - POOF! -
They were all gone – And Whitney and Grayson were gone too.
All sound stopped - All memory was gone - and there was nothing - anywhere.

Then, Whitney and Grayson woke up in the strawberry field.
They rubbed their eyes and shook their heads - because they were kind of sleepy and confused.

Grayson said, yawning, "Whitney, what happened? - did we fall asleep after eating strawberries?"

Whitney said, "I don't know – but I think I remember a dream.
But, inside - I feel like, I know, that it wasn't a dream!
Grayson said, "That's weird! - me too!"

They began to talk about their "dream" experiences - And they remembered the Woodland Angels - And all of their new friends - And all the life mysteries they had learned.

They thought everything they were remembering was all so amazing - they didn't' really care how it happened.
They were grateful they got to experience it - And all their new friends!

They figured they had better head home - because it was getting kind of late - so they stood up to leave the strawberry field.
But then, they noticed something about each other.

They saw that they both - had sparkling emerald green fairy dust - all over their clothes!

Then, they saw silver, gold, and violet Angel dust - sparkling all over the ground around them!
Then, they noticed there were tiny pieces of Angel dust - shaped like musical notes - in their hair!

Now, they knew for sure - that what they experienced - was absolutely not a dream!
They both just looked at each other - And smiled a great big happy smile.

Then, they were drawn to look up at the sky.
They saw the most beautiful red fog - move across the sky.
Whitney and Grayson knew inside - this was a sign from Archangel Michael - And that the Angels were near.

They both had an inside knowing, a gut feeling you know.
 They knew their lives were going to be so different now.

Grayson said, "Well, Whitney - the Angels did say - they would show us signs and give us knowing!
And they did say - that they would always be near - to help us understand.
And yep, it's all true!

They looked up to the sky one more time before leaving. This time, they saw two very bright stars twinkling - high up in the sky.
And they knew inside that it was the Magical Woman and Wizard Mitch.

Then they heard them whisper through the sky - They said, together -
"Don't ever forget the greatness you were born with Little Angels -
And remember to share your greatness with all living things."

Whitney and Grayson thanked them - And then blew a bunch of loving kisses to them.

Then, they heard a beautiful voice - singing a sweet lullaby through the entire sky - And they knew inside - that it was Lauralisa, Mother Universe.

Whitney and Grayson didn't even have to say anything to each other - because they knew they were both thinking the same thing.
They weren't ready to go home - just yet.

So they decided to be kind and loving to themselves - And receive all the perfect, beautiful, magical energy - that was happening around them.

Whitney and Grayson laid back down in the strawberry field.

They closed their eyes - And opened their hearts with love - as they listened to Mother Universe sing her beautiful lullaby to them.

As her heavenly voice moved through them - they knew without a doubt - they would always be perfect - just the way they are.

The End

~ Or ~

Is it the Beginning
of a magical new way of thinking
about life?!

DRAWING AND COLORING FRIENDS

Draw your own picture of the Magical Woman of the Forest.
What does she look like in your mind?

Draw your own picture of the Magical Wizard, Mitch.

Draw your own picture of the old, ancient tree and magic carpet.

Draw your own picture of Archangel Michael.

Draw your own picture of the floaty bubble things, fairy dust, shadows, mists, and swirls.

Draw your own picture of the Makaiya Ladybugs, Jessica Fairies, Ryan earthworms, and Jacob glow-worms.

Draw your own picture of the Aaliyah butterflies and the Jonah honey bees.

Draw your own picture of the Payton flowers and Brooklyn bunnies.

Draw your own picture of Archangel Uriel.

Draw your own picture of the Allison raccoons and Emily foxes.

Draw your own picture of the Sophia deer, Rylee doves, and Miranda Ruby phoenix.

Draw your own picture of the Adamcarl owl.

Draw your own picture of Archangel Raphael.

Draw your own picture of the Godderic turkeys.

Draw your own picture of the Shawnshawn squirrels.

Draw your own picture of the Earth Spirit Geri, the Wind Spirit Jennifer, the Water Spirit Boni, and the Fire Spirit Faith.

Draw your own picture of Archangel Gabriel.

Draw your own picture of Lauralisa Mother Universe.

As you learn and grow in life -

may you always...

Shine your love,

Speak your truth

Live in togetherness

and Share your joyous child heart

with every living thing you meet!

Other Books By Jennifer

To ascend consciousness away from the suffering mentality is a lifelong process that takes time and great devotion.

Having experienced the ascension process personally, I have shared the physical and spiritual transitions in a series of five books to initiate the process and ease through life's experiences.

In order of ascension steps, the series is heightened and best received in the following order: Emerge, Woodland Angels, Infinite Wellness, The Garden, and Life Beyond Us.

Life Beyond Us - *An eclectic, mind-blowing memoir of heartwarming and mysterious spiritual experiences with the afterlife.*

Woodland Angels - *A comforting, magical life guide for children and adults helping to see life challenges in other ways.*

Infinite Wellness - *An all encompassing wellness guide based on natural living and functional wellness for the body, mind, and spirit.*

Emerge - *An eye-opening self-help practice guide to overcome self-undoing limitations.*

Fur Babies Speak - *A heart-warming journal of signs and mysteries shared with my pets in the great beyond.*

The Garden - *An inspiring handbook of quotes reflecting life thoughts to ponder for higher consciousness.*

Jennifer Bryant
https://jenniferbryantholisticwriter.wordpress.com

Made in the USA
Middletown, DE
07 November 2021